a
woman
determined

Jean Swallow

Spinsters Ink
Duluth, MN

"For Strong Women" from *The Moon is Always Female* by Marge Piercy, ©1980 by Marge Piercy, reprinted by permission of Alfred A. Knopf Inc.

First edition published September, 1998 by Spinsters Ink
10-9-8-7-6-5-4-3-2-1

Spinsters Ink
32 E. First St., #330
Duluth, MN 55802-2002 USA

Cover illustration and design by Sara Sinnard, Sarin Creative

Production:

Liz Brissett	Kim Riordan
Helen Dooley	Emily Soltis
Joan Drury	Amy Strasheim
Tracy Gilsvik	Liz Tufte
Marian Hunstiger	Nancy Walker
Claire Kirch	Cheryl Wall
Marian Michener	

Library of Congress Cataloging-in-Publication Data
Swallow, Jean.
    A woman determined / Jean Swallow. — 1st ed.
       p.   cm.
    ISBN 1-883523-28-1 (alk. paper)
    I. Title.
PS3569.W23W66   1998
813'.54—dc21   98–27966
                                         CIP

Printed in the USA on recycled acid-free paper

Acknowledgments

The author would like to thank the following generous individuals for their financial, editorial, emotional, and/or technical support during the long creation of this project: Lesley Anderson, Nicholas Carter, Bob Dean, Mary Pat Hough, Ron Lindeau, Marty Mattox, Beth MacLeod, Marian Michener, Gary Moss, Marj Plum, Susan Sanford, Ellen Shapiro, Roz Solomon, Gordon Smyth, Diane Spaugh, Scott Stalnaker, the Three, Julia Velson, the best editor in the world, Wendy Williams, and the woman who read every single word of every single draft and always asked for more, my partner, Betsy Walker.

Editor's Note

Jean Swallow thought of *A Woman Determined* (she called it *A Cure for Bitterness*) as a fictional experiment and was not convinced, before her death in 1995, that it worked. A year later, in 1996, I did a reading at a bookstore in Seattle and was approached by Jean's good friend and literary heir, Marian Michener, about this book. Because I was familiar with Jean's work and liked it, I encouraged Marian to send us the manuscript.

And here it is, all of us disagreeing with Swallow's initial apprehension regarding her book's workability. We at Spinsters are proud and pleased to be presenting Jean's final novel to her devoted fans (as well as garnering new fans).

It's strange, editing the book of a deceased author. On the one hand, it seemed like it would be a "breeze"—*because the writer would not be arguing with me*. On the other hand, it seemed like I couldn't change ANYTHING—*because the writer would not be arguing with me*. And yet . . . every book needs some editing, some shaping, some illumination.

The vast majority of editing was simple punctuation and grammatical alterations. In the few instances when text was modified--a word or phrase altered or added or deleted, it was done with the intention of achieving clarity. I had the great good fortune of receiving input, encouragement, and support from Marian Michener and Jean's partner, Betsy Walker. All of us were dedicated to maintaining the integrity of Jean's original work and respecting her intentions, style, and characters' voices.

I think we accomplished these goals and wish Jean were here, both to let us know (argue with us, even) and to receive the rewards of a well-done creation.

—Joan M. Drury, 1998

For Strong Women

by Marge Piercy, 1980

A strong woman is a woman who is straining.
A strong woman is a woman standing
on tiptoe and lifting a barbell
while trying to sing Boris Godunov.
A strong woman is a woman at work
cleaning out the cesspool of the ages,
and while she shovels, she talks about
how she doesn't mind crying, it opens
the ducts of the eyes, and throwing up
develops the stomach muscles, and
she goes on shoveling with tears
in her nose.

A strong woman is a woman in whose head
a voice is repeating, I told you so,
ugly, bad girl, bitch, nag, shrill, witch,
ballbuster, nobody will ever love you back,
why aren't you feminine, why aren't
you soft, why aren't you quiet, why
aren't you dead?

A strong woman is a woman determined
to do something others are determined
not be done. She is pushing up on the bottom
of a lead coffin lid. She is trying to raise
a manhole cover with her head, she is trying
to butt her way through a steel wall.
Her head hurts. People waiting for the hole
to be made say, hurry, you're so strong.

A strong woman is a woman bleeding
inside. A strong woman is a woman making
herself strong every morning while her teeth
loosen and her back throbs. Every baby,
a tooth, midwives used to say, and now
every battle a scar. A strong woman
is a mass of scar tissue that aches
when it rains and wounds that bleed
when you bump them and memories that get up
in the night and pace in boots to and fro.

A strong woman is a woman who craves love
like oxygen or she turns blue choking.
A strong woman is a woman who loves
strongly and weeps strongly and is strongly
terrified and has strong needs. A strong woman is strong
in words, in action, in connection, in feeling;
she is not strong as a stone but as a wolf
suckling her young. Strength is not in her, but she
enacts it as the wind fills a sail.

What comforts her is others loving
her equally for the strength and for the weakness
from which it issues, lightning from a cloud.
Lightning stuns. In rain, the clouds disperse.
Only water of connection remains,
flowing through us. Strong is what we make
each other. Until we are all strong together,
a strong woman is a woman strongly afraid.

Dedication

for LJA
for giving so much to so many, not the least of whom was me

Note to the Reader

This book consists of a series of twenty matched interviews, ten with the former administrator of Seattle's Hull House Women's Clinic, Margaret Donovan, and ten more with her attorney, Laura Gilbert. The interviews were done in conjunction with a series of articles designed to profile the unrecognized women who have built our community institutions; however, it became very clear early on that this particular series of interviews would be, of the subjects' own volition, focused on other events. It was felt best to split these interviews off from the larger story and to publish them separately.

This book is a work of fiction and, although the author hopes you believe the events recorded here actually happened, she would like to remind you that the characters live entirely as acts of imagination, and any similarities to real people, living or dead, is purely coincidental.

Years Have Passed

Margaret Donovan

It's unfortunate you were late. I'm not sure how much time I have to talk with you now.

I understand. I apologize for my lateness. Could we get started, go as far as we can, and perhaps continue later?

We'll have to see. Maybe you can tell me a little more about what this is all about.

Well, as I said at the reception, I feel strongly that the women in the lesbian community who have built our institutions have been unrecognized for too long by most of the women who use those institutions. Now that there's a whole new generation of women coming along, it seemed important to record how we got to where we are. I'm doing a series of stories profiling lesbians who have made a difference. I wanted to talk with you about your work with Hull House.

I see. Have you talked with anyone else yet?

Yes, I have several interviews already completed.

No, I mean about me and Hull House.

Yes. At the reception there were a number of women who each had pieces of the history of the clinic, and I was able to set up interviews with some others . . .

Did anyone talk about why I left the clinic? Or mention Annie Bartleby, by chance?

Several people had different versions of the story. That's one of the things I'd like to talk with you about. It sounded like a difficult time for you.

It was. Have you talked with Annie Bartleby?

No. Not yet.

But you're going to, aren't you?

There are a number of people I'd like to talk with.

Well, I just want it known I was not the one who brought this all up again. Make sure you write that down. I did not drag this garbage to the surface. But if you're going to talk with her, you'd better talk to me, because you're never going to get the whole story from her. Annie Bartleby could not tell the truth if her life depended on it. She distorts events, makes up things that never happened; she says people said things they didn't. She even changes what she herself said. She's completely unreliable and I just want you to remember that when you interview her.

I will certainly try to keep it in mind. As long as we are talking about it, maybe we could just start here, and you could tell me how you came to leave the clinic.

How I came to leave the clinic? Well, it's a long story.

How about the brief version?

Okay, briefly now, I don't want to spend a lot of time on this, very briefly, there was an undetected embezzling scheme going on that I discovered only after a sizable amount of money had been taken, enough to almost kill the clinic. Due to some health problems, I was unable to give the clinic my full attention to deal with the situation. Over time, my health problems did not resolve themselves, and I resigned so the clinic could hire someone who could adequately address the issues that had come up. I was very sorry to have to leave.

Well, that seems simple enough. How difficult it must be to have rumors still floating around after four years.

I beg your pardon?

Well, my understanding of what happened is that you were involved in the scandal only insofar as you were the clinic administrator who discovered the money was missing. But surely you must be aware of the rumors.

Well, this takes the cake! You meet me at a dinner given in my honor, flatter me, say you would like to interview me about the early days of the clinic, and you look like part of the community, so I agree. Then you get here, thirty minutes late, and I find out what you really want to talk about is Annie Bartleby's embezzlement. Are you now implicating me in that somehow? I'll say one thing. You have a lot of nerve.

I am terribly sorry. I certainly did not mean to distress you. I assumed you had heard the rumors. As you know, I have been interviewing other people at non-profits and elsewhere who have mentioned your name, but I have not supposed that you are, in fact, in any way implicated. Still, there are rumors, and I'd like to get them cleared up. Wouldn't you?

I don't know what you are talking about.

The clinic almost had to close in 1990, due to a severe financial crisis. I wanted to talk with you about how you started and ran the clinic, but, unfortunately, rumors about that crisis seem to have clouded some people's vision of your work there. This story might be a good place to clear up some misconceptions. People gossip when the truth is unavailable.

People gossip whenever they get the chance. Still, I see your point. What have you heard?

I've heard a number of different stories. Some people have said, as you have, that an employee embezzled so much of the operating funds, the clinic was bankrupt and only the efforts of people like yourself saved it. Other people have said to me they never really knew what happened, but that you left the clinic shortly after the funds were found missing.

That's a lie. That's a bald-faced lie.

And some people say that you mismanaged contract funding so much that the clinic nearly went under, and you were forced to resign by going out on a chemical dependency disability.

I can't believe this.

And there are still others who say they knew the clinic needed money, and you made a fundraising appeal which they gave to, and then, suddenly, you weren't at the clinic. You were nowhere to be found. No one saw you for more than a year, and then you surfaced, you owned a home in Fremont, which no one could figure out how you could afford.

Like it's any of their goddamn business! This is really outrageous! *None* of this is true. What happened at the clinic was really very simple. Someone stole from us. Everything else you heard is slander. Vicious slander. I can't imagine why people would say these things, but I bet if you traced them all down, you'd find a single source. Annie Bartleby.

Do you know other people I could talk with who could support your perspective? It would strengthen the story, so I would like to talk with them. If you could help me out with names —people who were there, who have first-hand knowledge . . .

I'll tell you one person who can clear a lot of this up is Barbara Chadwick.

Barbara Chadwick would not talk on record with me.

Well, that's weird. Maybe she doesn't trust journalists. But then, you're not doing a story on her. Barbara somehow manages to stay . . . never mind.

I suppose you could talk with a woman who was my attorney at the time, although I hate to bring her into this. But she could certainly confirm most of what I'm going to tell you. Terrible attorney, although she doesn't lie, not that I know of. You could talk with her. Laura Gilbert. I don't know what she's doing now; she's not practicing law. You'd have to dig her up. Dammit.

I'll find her. Look, I certainly did not mean to upset you. I assumed you had heard these things. I am not trying in any way to implicate you. I would be happy to talk with your attorney or anyone else if you feel that would help me understand what happened. I would just like to get a full picture of you and the clinic. One thing I heard was that you had a terrible accident right about the time you left. Is that the health problem you were referring to?

Yes. Not that it has anything to do with this. I had a bad accident from which I have yet to and may never completely recover. I was run down by a car. But I still don't see what this has to do with the clinic or the embezzlement or any of it.

I'd like to be able to see where you were and where the clinic was, what was happening with you then. I'd like to be able to understand what you are going to tell me, to put it in the context of your life and the life of the clinic. Usually rumors come from stories people have only heard part of, so they make up the rest. If you could, I think it would help if you'd tell me what happened the day you got hit.

I still don't see what this has to do with anything, but sure, I'll tell you. I don't have anything to hide. I'm not the one with something to hide. People who spread these rumors—why didn't they just ask me? I would have told them exactly what happened. You'd think they didn't have enough to do.

If you could tell me, I could tell all of them through the story. Do you remember the day you got hit?

God, you've really got me between a rock and a hard place. I resent this intrusion into my private life, and I want you to note that. I don't think what I do in my private life is anybody's business, and I'm angry I have to talk about it, just because somebody in the community is slandering me. I resent it, and I won't forget it.

But I suppose I should talk with you. Sometimes I wonder

if there will ever be an end to this. I get so sick of Annie Bartleby. Goddammit.

Yes, I remember the day I got hit very well. No matter what has happened since, or what might happen to me years from now, I'll never forget that day. It seems now like a movie I've seen a million times.

Even at the time it happened, it felt like a movie; it felt like I was above the whole scene watching and part of me kept thinking, God, this is awful, why doesn't somebody do something?

Sometimes, I lay in bed before sleep, and I think about that day and how it utterly changed my life. To tell you the truth, getting hit by a car driven by a doctor . . . Now I want you to try to imagine this: a doctor who didn't even get out of the car to see how I was, to see if I was . . . try to see this. I'm lying in the street. I can't get up. There is a crowd around me. I am in screaming pain. I mean to say, I *am* screaming. And the man who hit me, who could have helped me, sat in his car without lifting a finger except to call the police and, we found out later, his attorney.

Try to understand that, for me, getting hit by Dr. Harry Brice changed my life much more than finding out Annie Bartleby embezzled from the women's clinic. That was bad for the clinic. Getting run down by a car was bad for *me*.

Did you see me walk in this room? Did you notice? I still can't walk right, and I never will be able to walk like a normal person again. I can not run if I need to. I am never safe, do you understand that? I can not go out at night. If I fall in the middle of the night, and can not get up, there will be nothing I can do. I have almost constant pain, and it's a pain I have to live with. Do you think with constant pain I would forget the day I got hit? I'll never forget the day I got hit.

Brice hit me directly on my left knee and hard enough to throw me to the other side of the street. He didn't even get out of the car. My knee was shattered. Bone in fragments like crumbled blue cheese, my surgeon said. Months, months I was in physical therapy, three times a week. And in terrible pain. I couldn't do my work. I couldn't supervise. I couldn't get out of bed for weeks.

You want perspective? Fine. This is my perspective. I haven't thought about Annie Bartleby in years. I think about my knee every hour of every day. Do you understand?

I'm trying to understand. Can you tell me what happened the day you got hit?

My God, you're tenacious, aren't you? Even Brice's thug lawyers weren't this tenacious at the mediation. They were just scum who left slime on anything they got near. Attorneys. You've heard that joke, haven't you? What's the difference between a catfish and an attorney? One is a pond-dwelling, scum-sucking, bottom-feeder, and the other is a fish?

I have heard that joke, and I still think it's funny. But I'm not a lawyer. I'm not trying to make a case against you. I'm writing a story about you and Hull House. Part of that story seems to be about how you left. I would like to bring your perspective on that to the community that should be honoring you. I'm hoping you'll help me find out what happened to you and Hull House.

Okay. I'm sorry. I don't mean to bark at you, but you really took me off guard with those rumors. I honestly had never heard all of them, although, maybe I had some idea; I mean things make sense now, knowing that. And I get impatient when people are late. I know you're not an attorney. I see that you are not the same. Your shoes aren't expensive enough, for one thing.

There, good. I finally got a smile out of you. So, okay. What was the question? What did I do that day? Before he hit me, you mean? Well, let me see. Yes. I can remember it. I can remember all of it.

I'd spent the morning getting ready for a block grant review meeting downtown at the City Health Department. They had asked us to submit a request for proposal for new services, which I had done and sent in the week before. Then this queen—excuse my language, but he was—this queen called me up and said he wanted to go over the accounting on the first major block grant we had gotten from the city, which was coming up for fiscal-end review.

So I set up a meeting with him, and I was dreading it. See, we had been receiving the money he wanted to talk about for about two and a half years, and the final audits were due. I was anxious about it, because I didn't really know how that was done. I hate to admit this, but it's the truth. Annie Bartleby had set the books up on that grant, and all the grants we'd gotten up to that point. I hadn't ever paid too much attention to what Annie was doing, which was my fatal error. I mean, if she tries to say I had something to do with the embezzlement, she's right.

I didn't watch her closely enough. I didn't pay attention to what she was doing. That's what I did wrong. I didn't watch her. I didn't think I needed to. I never dreamed, well, maybe I should have seen it coming, but I didn't.

She was my lover. I'm sure you've heard that, although probably not from her. The way she left me, you'd think she was ashamed to have ever been seen with me. She left me—and the clinic I might add—six months before that meeting. To the day, as I recall, which did not improve my mood when I went to see the Queen of the City books. Would you like some coffee? I can make us a fresh pot. I think I still know how to run this machine. No? Well, I think I'll just make myself a cup. I get cold since the accident; my knee, feel it. It's like an iceberg.

Okay, try to understand this. The thing about Annie Bartleby was, when she left me, she just stopped doing the clinic books overnight. She never came back. Just like that. That should have told me something, but at the time, we were so totally helpless I didn't really notice. She made some noises about how she would come back and finish up, but only if she were paid what she called "compensation" for all the work she'd done. Give me a fucking break. Like anyone who ever worked in the clinic got adequately "compensated" for all the hours they put in there. Well, I can tell you, looking back on it, I probably should have paid a lot of attention to that.

Because where was she going to get money to start this new life of hers? I knew she needed it. It's expensive to split up after five years. She had to start over, security deposit on a new apartment, first and last rent, that sort of thing. We had hardly any money to speak of in our joint checking account, and most of that I had taken out because it was mine. She needed money just to move her things from our house to her new apartment. And she knew, she must have known by then, since she'd obviously been draining it off, that the clinic had the potential for petty cash, at least. The clinic never had much money. If we'd had any money to begin with, we'd have gotten a half-decent bookkeeper who didn't skim off the top.

But at the time, I couldn't figure out where she got the money even to buy a new bed for her new life in her new apartment. Well, it became clear soon enough where the money came from, and where it had been coming from. In a way, you know, the embezzlement didn't turn out to involve what most people would call a lot of money, although to us it was, and to have stolen any at all from us, from a women's community clinic, is beyond me. To this day, I still don't understand how she could have done that to us.

But what was really bad, for me, was that I let it happen at all. I didn't watch her. I didn't know how she'd set up the books. I had no idea, honestly, no idea that she had commingled funds from the different funding sources we had in those days. To tell you the truth, I didn't even know what commingling funds meant. All I knew was that I had not done my job. I had trusted someone who wasn't trustworthy, someone who was my lover no less.

Could you explain commingling to me?

Well, if you want to know the truth, even now it seems

arcane, but it has to do with keeping grant monies separate. Like if you got grant A for one service and grant B to provide a different service, you couldn't use money from grant B to do the work for grant A, even if you were only covering a cash flow problem. Now, for this to really make sense, I want you to think of just one thing. Light bulbs.

Excuse me?

Light bulbs. You have to have lights. Every office needs lights—during the day as well as night. But it's especially important in a clinic like ours because we provide a full range of services during our night hours. So many of our patients, you know, can't get there during the day. So who pays for the light bulbs? You see? You have to be able to have an accountant who can divide a light bulb. We didn't. And that's what I found out the day I got hit.

Now that I think about it, I got hit twice that day. First by that screaming queen, pointing out and defining commingling to me that afternoon, and then later, when Dr. Brice was traveling too fast—now think about this—traveling too fast on Broadway to stop for a pedestrian. He really had to work at that. I suppose we are all lucky he didn't kill someone. Sometimes, to tell you the truth, I wish he had.

So, you'd been at this meeting, and . . .

And, I was tired. I remember that. I'd spent the entire morning trying to prepare for the meeting, poring over the books Annie had left. I could follow some of it, and my friend Barbara Chadwick, who really is an accountant and was president of the board, had come down and that's when we began to realize something was really wrong. I don't know what I would have done without Barbara.

She's on the clinic board still. Actually, now that I'm thinking about it, Annie had introduced us. Annie had been working for Barbara before she went out on her own, and now I remember, that's why I called Barbara that morning, to see if she could help us out. I hoped she would be able to figure out

Annie's system which, to tell you the truth, was a mystery to me.

See, in the early days of the clinic, we didn't have enough money to go out and hire someone to do the books. Annie was a bookkeeper and said she would do it to help. And, frankly, I appreciated it. In those days, I was doing everything—from washing the equipment at night to assisting the NP's during clinic hours. We did all the billing by hand. Do you have any idea what I'm talking about?

Could you explain it to me?

It was a very small clinic, very young. We were only three years old at the time I met Annie, struggling along. We had only one paid part-time nurse practioner and me. That's it. I took the appointments. I did the scheduling. I made copies of the forms after I designed them. I filed the patient charts. I begged the doctors into coming down one night a week for free. I figured out how to get us all paid, finally. I built the place; I mean, I literally put together the cheap furniture on the weekends. This clinic didn't get to be here because some government agency came in and set us up. Do you think the government really cares what happens to women and their bodies? You think, I mean, where do you think this clinic came from?

I thought probably lesbians built it. That's why I wanted to do a story about it. And you. I want people to know where it came from.

Thank you. Yes, lesbians built it—with their sweat and blood. Mine, mostly.

And did you discover the missing money that day?

No, that day I just discovered that there was something wrong. When we were going over the books that day, Barbara said she didn't know how we were going to pay the bills that month without commingling funds. Well, I was horrified. First of all, I had never heard the term commingle, but I knew it was not good because it sounded sexual, and sex and money are never good in the same sentence. And second, I knew then that

Annie had done something really, really wrong. I remember, all that day I had a sinking feeling, kind of a dread in my stomach, like someone had a giant hand pressing down on me, and I couldn't get away. It was a kind of gray day, I remember, early winter, you know those November days when you realize winter has come, that fall is really over?

I'm sorry, I'm not from here.

Well, it doesn't matter. It's just, well, it was a gray day, and I was feeling anxious and heavy, pinned down, like the way the air feels in February. First, it was the books and Barbara all morning saying, "This doesn't look good," and "What happened here?" which, of course, I couldn't answer. Then it was this asshole faggot lording it over me during the meeting. I'm telling you, I could have leaned across the desk and choked his skinny little neck with his skinny little leather tie. I could have. That kind of man inspires me, really.

And another thing, now that I think about it, I was having hot flashes all afternoon. And I could tell this jerk was just sitting there thinking up menopausal women jokes to tell his buddies. I could just tell, every time I took my sweater on and off. It was his smirk. I was not in a good mood coming back to the office.

I remember traffic was slow, and my car stalled a couple of times; I still had the Chevy in those days. Annie had left with the Honda, and I needed to get the Chevy tuned up, but I didn't have the money, and I didn't have the time, and I was cursing her too, as I recall. So I was pretty mad by the time I got out of the car. My run-in with Dr. Brice did nothing to improve my sense of humor, I can tell you that.

What happened exactly?

It was pretty simple. It was about quarter of five. I found a parking space almost right across the street from the pizza place, only about a block from the clinic, which was a miracle because there is *never, ever* any parking near the clinic. Anyway, I got out, got my papers and my briefcase, unbuttoned my raincoat because I was hot again, and locked the car. I turned around and started across the street. He was speeding. I never saw him coming.

I never knew what hit me. Honestly. I heard tires squealing, and then I heard this noise, like a crunching sound. And then, the next thing I knew, I was on the ground, and there were folks all around me, and I tried to answer them, but I couldn't get the words to form. And then someone, a woman I remember, asked me if there was anyone she could call for me and all I could think of was my home number, and I couldn't, well, there was no one there anymore, you see, and I . . .

That's okay. Take your time.

Well, finally, I remembered the clinic number. But just then, the paramedics came, and I remember screaming at them not to touch me. It's funny, I don't remember the pain, not then. I just knew, somehow, I knew I couldn't stand up. And I knew I didn't want anyone touching me. If it hadn't been for Barbara Chadwick, who finally came out of the clinic to see what all the commotion was, I don't know if those guys would have ever gotten me into the ambulance, although I was bleeding. I suppose at some point I would have passed out, but anyway, Barbara came and talked me through it.

I ended up in the hospital lying on a gurney, alone in a corridor at Central, waiting to be seen. Seattle Central may be the best place for trauma, but it wasn't for me. By the time they got around to examining me, my knee had swollen so they really couldn't tell what was going on, even with X-rays. So they washed out my superficial wounds and gave me pain meds and sent me home. To sleep. Like I could.

You couldn't sleep?

I can see I'm not making myself clear here. It was the most intense pain of my life. My tibial plateau was shattered. Do you understand that?

Not exactly.

Well, the knee is actually a very simple ball and socket

joint. The ball of the femur, your thigh bone, rests in the socket of the tibia, your lower leg bone, and is held there by some muscles. The knee cap floats over the joint. The socket part of the joint is called the tibial plateau. Mine was gone. Every time I tried to move, tried to get up to go to the bathroom or get something to read or just roll over, it was awful. Just lying there was awful. The pain meds were awful. The whole thing was one long nightmare.

So what happened?

Well, I lay at home for a couple of days, as instructed, waiting for the swelling to go down, which it never did, trying to do my work, trying to supervise the office from home. By that time, we had a receptionist, a back-office clerk we had hired after Annie left, two full-time medical assistants, two nurse practitioners, and a part-time medical director, an MD. They were calling me for things like finding out where the letterhead was stored. I was out of my mind, and they wanted to know where the stationery was. Finally, I got in to see a real orthopedist who took me directly to surgery. But that was almost a week later.

So I lay there that week, and all my friends came to take care of me. They were great. And I lay there, and I can tell you, that was the last time I really thought much about Annie Bartleby. Honestly. When I discovered the embezzlement, I thought about her, but I didn't care anymore. It was a clinic problem. It wasn't my problem anymore. She never called once to see how I was, by the way, and I know she knew about it. But, it's all water under the bridge as far as I'm concerned. What I can't believe is how other people haven't let it go; I know all those rumors came from Annie. You'd think she'd be over it by now, not still fanning the flames. I mean, come on. Years have passed. But I suppose some things never change.

Laura E. Gilbert

I remember very well the first day I met Margaret Donovan. During our regular lunch the week before, my old friend and former partner in crime, Audrey Carr, had told me to expect a call from Margaret, and in fact, she did call. I arranged to meet her at her house since she was unable to come to my office, which was not something I usually did, and perhaps I should have assigned some meaning to that at the time, but I didn't.

I knew of Margaret, of course, everyone did. She was one of those women—well, names get around, even in the lesbian communities where we are governed not only by the rules of the larger culture (where girls should be seen, but not heard) but also by the politics of our own communities which are largely feminist and, as such, opposed to patriarchal hierarchy, so we say we have no "stars." Human nature being what it is, of course, there are always women who, in another time, would have been said to have "done good works." And we all know who they are, even if we don't always honor them or recognize their achievements.

Maybe it's only because Seattle is, in so many ways, such a small town, but within the first six months of sitting through board meetings of any women's or lesbian non-profit or some lesbian committee or other, a person would know who was whom. You would know at least the names of our own movers and shakers: those women who were known by reputation for what they had done and how much they gave to the community, how many evenings they gave up to meetings, how much responsibility they shouldered for how little money (which has always seemed to have a directly inverse ratio).

The gay men have written, sometimes bitterly, about A-list fags; well, we didn't have that. We have what my mother used to call "formidable women," and Margaret Donovan was definitely one of them. She was called the Mighty Meg, although not to her face, I don't believe. I can't even imagine anyone who would have dared call Margaret anything of the sort to her face, even as a joke. Margaret is not the kind of woman with whom you make jokes in that way, as I'm sure you've discovered.

Well. I can't tell you how surprised I am to have been asked to speak with you. I hope you don't mind my insisting on a signed privacy release from her. Sitting here with it in my hands, I'm still absolutely amazed that you got it. I suspect you have come to me to help you make sense of what happened. I hope I'll be able to help you. I don't know that I can, but you are welcome to my thoughts.

Yes, Margaret was one of my clients and usually during a case such as hers, I would get to know a client fairly well. That was something on which I prided myself, and one of the few things that made private practice interesting, even up until the end. I suppose this is another example of pride preceding the fall. In any event, I did represent Margaret Donovan, and although I did my best to help her, I have been told she harbors great resentment toward me to this day. Which is understandable, given her life. But I'm not certain I understood *her* at all. I wish I had.

I will say this though: Margaret Donovan has been subject to unfair rumors in this community, and if I can help clear the record on any of it, I will be happy to do so. I think the kind of story you are doing is very important, and I think it's long overdue. In my opinion, Margaret has done a great deal of very valuable work for this community, and my understanding is that she continues to do so, to this day. She has had some unfortunate times in her life, and she can be, at times, a difficult woman, but none of this can negate the value of her work.

Excuse me. That noise coming from the kitchen is my partner, Brenna, who is unloading groceries and doing her best not to let loose with her famously loud laughter. Brenna, come in here; show your face to this nice reporter. Kiss me and leave us alone, all right?

Brenna—thank you darling—Brenna has some unprintable opinions about Margaret, which we will not share with you. Go on now, but you must give her some allowance. She's my partner. She's supposed to defend me. I don't need defending, but I always appreciate her willingness to do so.

Where were we?

In many ways, Margaret Donovan has done great things and with very little support. She nursed into strength the only women's health clinic in this city, and she did it with no capital and no organized community support. She did it at a time when multicultural was a word that had not even been invented yet. Hull House Women's Clinic is known, not just in Seattle, but all over the country for innovative delivery of accessible health care for all women—including lesbians, immigrants, poor, and working women across class and cultural backgrounds. While the original vision might not have been Margaret's, it was her commitment that made Hull House happen, and for that work alone she deserves recognition from us all.

But she has also worked tirelessly in organizing the lesbian community and not just around health care. She's been active on the boards of several different non-profits and attended countless strategy meetings of different political groups and different combinations of coalitions. I had noticed, for a long time, that her name was always on the list of volunteers who made numerous events possible, and I would like to say that, for me, counts as much as the names you always see on the donor lists.

In the days before her accident, it was not uncommon to see Margaret breezing in, always late, with her raincoat blossoming out behind her like a great cape. She has a big voice, and she is a big woman with a lot of energy, and she often seemed to be everywhere at once. I watched her work a room one time at a fundraising party, about six months before I became her attorney, and I remember being fascinated by her and by her bright red earrings. I couldn't take my eyes off her. She had a laugh as bright as her earrings, and I wanted to know who she was, but I also wanted only to watch her. I didn't want to get too close. I suppose that says as much about me as it does about her, but then, you did ask me for background, by which I assume you mean mine as well.

At that particular lunch when Audrey first told me to expect a call from Margaret, I didn't have to be reminded who she was. I remembered her. I don't often remember women from that kind of community gathering, a part of my work that I truly detested. But I remembered Margaret.

My lunch with Audrey that day was memorable for several reasons, but they all have come to coalesce, in my mind, around Margaret. I had come into the restaurant early, which was unusual for me, and I remember it was raining, of course, but it was winter rain, and I was cold already, even though it was only November. And I was sick of the Second Avenue Grill where Audrey and I had been lunching weekly for six years. And I was sick, I was sick to death of my work. I wanted out, and I remember spooning the foam off my latte and thinking, I will, I will tell Audrey today. I have to get out of this profession completely. I simply did not feel I could be an attorney in any way anymore.

Well, there were a lot of reasons, not the least of which was that I was sick of being in a system that is so adversarially based, no one can possibly win. The phrase "justice for all" seemed to mock me on a daily basis. In our system, there can only be justice for one party, the prevailing party. I was sick of writing letters threatening other people; I was sick of the extremes opposing parties would take to ensure a fictive "middle" judgment some equally fictive "fact-finder" would determine, and I was really, really sick of telling myself that it didn't matter if my clients were telling the truth or not, that what mattered was that I give them the best representation available.

Have you been in Seattle long? I thought not. Oh, the umbrella. People here don't use them; we just rust. Well, there is a name for the sky here—it's called oyster gray, and it is lovely and luminescent. The artists treasure it. I tell you this by way of helping you understand that I was wanting more shades of gray in my life and less black and white that the court system fosters. I needed the ambiguities of real people, not the thin slivers of minutia out of which some believe you can build the truth, but which actually crumble like a toothpick house with the least pressure outside the practice of law.

Oh, I was so sick of it; I can't tell you. And I got sicker and sicker by the day, without the determination to really look at what was wrong. There were a lot of things I told myself so as not to know, but one night, about a month before I met Margaret, I caught myself saying to Brenna that I wished one of my clients would just take his $7,500 settlement, be glad I had been able to twist the system one more time for a bogus neck injury, quit his incessant whining, and get a real life.

I remember she looked at me, those big brown eyes dark and troubled, and I looked at her just as hard. She was in bed, sheet gathered around her neck as though she were afraid, watching me brush my hair, which she liked to do every night. And I had my head bent to my knees while I brushed and talked my day over with her, which I liked to do every night, and I remember straightening up without a sound and watching the words hang in the air between us, and I knew without having to say another word that we both knew it was time for me to go. How could I possibly give people adequate representation with an attitude like that? Well, I couldn't. And I knew it, and Brenna knew it, and I wondered how I had gotten there, and what had happened to all my big dreams.

I got into bed, and Brenna held me, and we didn't talk. I just stared into the darkness until long after she had gone to sleep, and I wondered how I was going to get out and what I would do, but I didn't ever again wonder if I would. It was simply a question of when, how soon I could wind down, how quickly I could find other work, and what that work might be.

It was a troubling time for me in some ways, but in other ways, I felt very, very clear. And I knew, if I took Margaret Donovan's case, which I was sure I would because she deserved every last effort I could give her, I still knew it would be my last big case. And I should have told Audrey that the second she told me to expect a call from Margaret. But I didn't.

Audrey and I had shared a law office for nearly six years, during which time she had helped me become very successful. Audrey loved her work, and I loved to watch her love it. She could sell coal to a coalminer's daughter and that, coupled with a brain sharper and quicker than a logger's chain saw, made her good in all kinds of law.

I remember even now how much pleasure I got from watching her that lunch because the moment she came to the table, before she even had her coat off or her napkin unfolded, she had announced the news about Margaret. I never had the chance to tell her I wanted out. Or maybe I should say I didn't *take* the chance. It would have been better for all of us if I had, but I didn't. I couldn't; I felt that I couldn't, not then.

Audrey was excited, her fair Irish cheeks blown cold into bright redness, brighter than her hair, and her eyes glistened behind her glasses, and I remember exactly what she said.

"This will be the case that will set you up for life, kid. This is the one you've been waiting for. Truth and justice and the American way, by which I mean—money for the taking. This is Robin Hood, and I'm talking directly to you."

She was laughing. We were both laughing. It was an old joke between us. There are actually very few windfall cases in personal injury work, and it is only clients who think every case must be so. In personal injury work, as with most law practice, there is only the daily grind of phone calls and counseling and meetings and delays. Perhaps a letter gets written, or a case actually comes to trial; then there are conferences and meetings and delays and counseling done in the court hallway. The hours are endless, the detail screamingly overwhelming. Usually, we are able to get what the case is worth—sometimes more, sometimes less—but most often, in the general vicinity of what has become fairly standard, codified loss/reimbursement/compensation ratios.

But people have this idea that there are many big cases, hopefully including theirs, which will be for them like winning the Lotto, the key to the lock of their lives. And these clients also imagine that from their heartache and settlement money, their attorneys will skim off the top, getting rich off their pain. It was an image Audrey and I often played with, more to take the edge off how much people seemed to hate us than to ease my middle-aged disillusionment with my life, but it worked for me in that way, too.

In those days, when Audrey laughed, I laughed too, at least in part for the pleasure of watching her laugh. I couldn't help myself. I suppose I was a little in love with her. Or maybe it wasn't that exactly, and it wasn't exactly that I wanted to be her, not at all really. But I did want something she had, some sureness, some certainty, some deep knowledge that the world was hers to conquer, that there was, in fact, a key to the lock. It seemed to me then that she knew everyone, and she knew how to get anything done. And I wanted that. All my life I had wanted that, and I suppose I hoped that a little of her knowledge would rub off on me. I suppose in some ways it did.

But I don't know that I knew any of this then. I knew I wanted Audrey to like me. I was aware of a kind of sick feeling in my stomach when I had done something of which she disapproved. She was older than I, by about ten years, had been in practice that much longer, had been that much more successful. So there was that, too, because at the time, I was transitioning from a career in corporate law to a solo private practice, and it was not such an easy change as one might imagine.

But I'm not sure the professional aspects of our relationship were nearly as important to me as others. I think more than anything, I simply wanted Audrey to like me, and she did, and I was aware how good it felt to have her approval surrounding me, especially since I felt so little approval for what I was doing myself. I was beginning to understand that I had not become the person I wanted to become, and though I was still holding on to those who did like where I had gone, I was already saying good-bye.

So, I laughed with Audrey that lunch and said very little. When Audrey talked, there wasn't much space for anyone else to get airtime on the best days, but also, I didn't talk a lot during those luncheons because I was afraid I would make a mistake, say the wrong thing, and not be able to finish lunch for that sick feeling. So I listened. Listening was easy with Audrey. And Margaret Donovan's story was good.

Two days before, Margaret had been struck by a car, Audrey reported, struck by a 700-series new BMW driven by a middle-aged plastic surgeon. Struck in broad daylight. And the good doctor did not bother to get out of his car to help the injured.

This seemed to Audrey to be the most delicious. She rubbed her hands together as the roast chicken arrived (to this day, the Second Avenue Grill has the best and cheapest spit-roast chicken in Seattle, and Audrey had that for lunch every week). She rubbed her hands together and picked up her knife and fork and leaned over her plate and said to me, "Think what a jury is going to do with that! Oh, the public may hate attorneys in theory, but this plastic surgeon is going to know the meaning of impaled when you get done with him." With that, she speared her chicken and began tearing it off the bone.

I put my fork down and stared at my plate. Well, really, I thought, but didn't say out loud. I took a sip of my latte and looked at her, mildly I hoped. "And what makes you think I'm going to be representing Ms. Donovan?" I asked. "What makes you think Ms. Donovan wants representation?"

She pointed her chicken-filled fork at me as though it were her finger. "I'll tell you why, my friend," she said. "Because I know Barbara Chadwick, the president of Margaret's board, and I know her well. That's one reason. But the best reason is because I know that once Barbara has Margaret call you, and you meet with her, I know you two will just hit it off, and she will want you to represent her. After all," she paused for emphasis; Audrey Carr is one of Seattle's great litigators, always has been and always will be. "After all, Margaret will want you to represent her because she won't be able to find a better lesbian personal injury attorney even if she looked hard. Which she won't. Because you'll already be there."

She smiled at me and went on eating. I sipped what was left of my latte and watched her. And I did not say a word. I thought to myself, well, okay, one more. Because it was Margaret Donovan, and because it was a good case. But that was it, I swore to myself. Maybe, I thought, maybe she wouldn't call. Or maybe there wasn't a case to be made. There is always that. You can't believe everything you hear. You never really know what happened anyway, but in the beginning you certainly can't make any assumptions, no matter who told you the story first, until you've spent some time with the client. I'd been at it long enough to know the cases that sounded clear and clean upon first telling were very often the cases that were full of ambiguity, and sometimes, not a small amount of duplicity.

I remember shrugging my shoulders, a self-reassuring motion I picked up from my twelve-year-old stepson Joe (no one makes a better shrug than a boy on the cusp of adolescence). Well, we'll see, I told myself, still thinking like a lawyer, focusing on the future and the immediate, both at once, hoping the call would not be made, and meanwhile, like the well-trained dog I was, off and running for the rabbit.

Of course, Margaret did call, said she'd gotten my name from Barbara Chadwick. There were times in my life as a lawyer when I felt like I was Audrey Carr's déja vu, and this was one of them. My first appointment with Margaret was during the very first week following her accident. Even now, I remember every detail.

Maybe I remember that meeting more than all the meetings with Margaret because it was the first. On the other hand, I remember most of them well because I had to describe them at length the following weeks while lunching with Audrey and was made to suffer through her cross-examination. When Audrey says she made me as a lawyer, that I was nothing until I met her, she's right. I learned more at those lunches than I learned in years of corporate law and certainly more than I ever learned in law school.

But you didn't come to talk with me about that. Let me tell you about the first time I saw Margaret. She lived in a classic Craftsman's bungalow, not restored, in the heart of Capital Hill. The house was dark, in need of repair and a paint-job. Margaret rented, so some of that can be explained, but even inside the house, as I remember, was moldy and gray and tumbled.

Tumbled. I mean, things in the hallway, old carpet covered with papers tumbling down from the piles they were stacked in, dishes teetering in the sink, clothing on the floor. That sort of thing. Tumbled. Margaret was not a housekeeper. That was fine. I didn't mind. I don't mean to say I didn't notice, but I didn't have judgments about it.

But there was something else, too, not just tumbled, but something abandoned there. I noticed one room, a front room off the hall which was closed, but no other room in the house had the door closed, and I remembered wondering what was in the closed room. I know now it was probably empty. In a way, the whole house felt empty, and I remember wondering if she was ever at home, if she actually lived there, or if she just changed clothes there on her way to somewhere else. It was the kind of place where old flowers stayed on the kitchen table weeks past dying, unnoticed.

Although there was none of that, dead flowers I mean, the day I met her. There were lots of flowers, but they were new or at least not yet dead. They crowded the kitchen table. Margaret was holding court in the living room, a room she had turned into the living room at any rate. It seemed to me to have probably been a dining room once, with a giant fir in the backyard and what looked like an extensive garden gone to seed.

I wasn't entirely sure where to sit because there were three cats on all the available chairs and two friends sitting on the floor next to her. Margaret was quite regal, with her leg propped up on the couch pillows and a wonderful old quilt draped over her, as though she were granting an audience. She was gracious to me, insisting one friend get the big black tom off the chair nearest to her. I remembered clearly the feeling I had when I watched her at the awards banquet: the sweeping hand motions, the laugh, the bigness of all of her.

I suppose I noticed, too, how her friends deferred to her, how they left us alone, and of course, I was grateful she made them go. I wasn't accustomed to meeting my clients with an audience. But I think I also noticed because I was aware of being alone with her and how intimate that felt, and I remember thinking to myself that I wished I'd had my big office desk between us. I didn't usually make house calls, and this was one of the reasons.

Still, she couldn't come to my office, obviously, and I was determined to offer her counsel. So what I did was, I told her the room seemed suddenly hot to me, and she laughed and said "Oh, you too. Please, for both of us then, open the windows!" And she laughed that bubble of a laugh, a laugh that seemed to start in her throat and then float merrily through the rest of her body, until she stopped it with a sigh. It was several years before I understood her laughter. Not until I got into menopause myself did I realize what she meant was probably harmless.

At the time, she made me very nervous, but then, it's always been hard for me to know if someone was coming on to me. Brenna says if she hadn't baldly stated her needs in a speech as persuasive as a jury summary, we never would have gone to bed together, and I suppose maybe she's right. Sometimes I think something is happening when it's not, too. I'm just not a good judge. Perhaps, like most of us, I never got enough practice as an adolescent.

My maneuver that day worked to put me at ease, however. When I sat back down from opening the window, I pulled my chair back a little and told myself I wanted to see my client's face better. I wanted to watch her and size her up for a jury. I wanted to see what they would see when they first saw her, and I wanted to see if there were a case to be made. My modus operandi in personal injury cases was to listen and watch while the injured told me their story. If I believed it, I knew I could make a jury believe it. I had done enough cases to feel secure in my estimation. Maybe Audrey wasn't just shooting the breeze when she said I was the best. I had done well by my clients.

It was just that I was beginning to doubt exactly what *was* doing well for my clients. Maybe it was because I had been in practice long enough to see the results of my labors, not just with the delivery of the verdict or even with the delivery of the check. I had kept in touch with a great many of my clients. And it wasn't just that I had begun to doubt what I was doing had anything to do with justice. I had wrestled with that angel for years. No, it was worse. I had begun to doubt that what I did for most of my clients had anything to do with helping them improve their lives.

Earlier that year, I had been at a party for professional

women, something Audrey suggested Brenna and I attend. For different reasons, it was a fairly excruciating experience for both of us; me for the memories it brought up and Brenna for the difference she felt. We were getting ready to leave when a doctor I had met once in court and who had earned my grudging respect, even though she had testified for the other side, came over to us. Perhaps she had had too much to drink, or perhaps a small amount of alcohol and a large amount of what looked like exhaustion had loosened her social inhibitions, but I couldn't leave when she asked me how the green-poultice-practice was coming along. Brenna tried to drag me away, but I was fascinated. Insulted but fascinated, and I asked the woman what she meant.

"Oh, you personal injury attorneys. Getting the green poultice treatment for your clients. I've seen your clients become healed, throw away their walking sticks, and cry 'hallelujah, hallelujah' when you put that poultice of green money on their wounds."

Brenna did succeed in dragging me away that night, but I wondered about what that doctor said for many nights after that, many nights and many client phone calls later. How *does* one measure what has been lost? What can be replaced? What can cure that which has been injured in us? In our culture, because it is a capitalist culture, we think money will do it. Or maybe, the cynical among us would say that we don't believe that, not really, but how else will we compensate someone for what they have lost? What other medium of exchange do we have? What else has meaning that we can trade among ourselves to make meaning?

I didn't know then, and I don't know now. In those days, the days when I first met Margaret, I was earnestly asking myself those questions and hoping, believing, I would find some answers, at least enough to allow me to continue to practice law until I could get my own house in order. And I remember sitting there with Margaret, thinking to myself that day, my God, nothing can make up for what has happened to her. The amount of pain she was in began to show very quickly, her face flushed, her breathing quickened, her knuckles tightened. I watched her bear her pain like a woman accustomed to it, and I wanted to say to her, Margaret, Margaret, let it go, scream it out if you need to, but all I said was, "Are they giving you enough pain meds?" and "When do you go back to the doctor?"

In what Audrey used to like to call my social worker way, I was able to get her in to see a real orthopedist immediately, the one who made the comment at the party, come to think of it, a really good doctor, and clearly an honest woman. It was not until two weeks later I began to wonder why Margaret seemed so accustomed to the pain. That first day, all I was able to do was to listen to her story. I remember taking notes and watching her face and her hands as she tightened and released, tightened and released the hem of the quilt she was clutching and I remembered thinking to myself, well, maybe I can help here.

I thought she had an open-and-shut case. And I will tell you, I didn't see how she could lose. She had tried to cross the street. To her great good luck, she was hit by a wealthy white male with insurance, probably very good insurance. She had been toiling in that clinic for years, making what I was sure was nothing near what she was worth. Maybe it wasn't God's justice she could get, and maybe it wasn't the revolution in health care that God knows this country needs, but I did believe we were going to be able to get her some compensation for her pain. I really did. And in those days, that was as close to justice as I could get for any of us. And I believed it was worth working for. I tried to push all the questions I had been having to the back of my mind and rolled up my sleeves.

Not So Far From Home

Margaret

So you're back. Well, I appreciate someone who's dedicated to their job. Were you able to find my attorney and get an appointment with her? Good. I guess. I must say, I was surprised last time at how much you wanted to focus on my private life. I hope this time we will be able to concentrate more on the clinic. I did not consent to these interviews to talk about my private life, which after all, is really no one's business. I agreed to talk about the embezzlement of funds from Hull House Women's Clinic in 1990, because it seemed important to me that other non-profits be made aware of what can happen. I did not agree to discuss my private life with you.

I understand. I hope you know I was only trying to get some background, some way to make sense of the rumors that have been filtering through the community for years. I was not trying to pry into your personal affairs. I just needed enough information so I could put the rumors in context, in order to dispel them. I thought we might start today with how you actually discovered that money was missing. Can you tell me what happened that day?

Well, actually it didn't happen on any one day. It unfolded over several weeks after I was hit. As soon as I could push through the pain meds long enough to get my head clear, I started working at least a little every day at home and then a little more the next day, then the next, and so on, until I was working about half-time. Which is to say, about eight hours a day! So it would have been, let's see, about two weeks after I got hit when I first began to really understand what had happened.

Let's say three weeks, just to make sure. That's almost a month, and frankly, I had been lying there all that time, brooding about how we were going to meet the payroll. To be honest, I was worried about how we were going to pay me *my* paycheck. Things were very tight for me then, because Annie had moved out and stuck me with the lease on the house, which was not cheap even when there were two of us there. She had wanted a place where she could garden, and then she just walked out on all of it. Which should give you some context for *her* story, whenever you talk with her.

Anyway, I was worried. Who wouldn't be? I didn't make any money working at the clinic; no one did, except Annie. I was running a clinic with a half-million dollar annual budget by then, but I was making what a medical secretary makes. I didn't have a new car. I didn't have nice clothes. I didn't have a VCR or any of those things. I had less than one month's salary in the bank, plus a little money Duke, my father, had left me when he died.

And I lay on the couch in those weeks, in terrific pain, and I thought about all that. My knee didn't seem to be getting better; many days it actually felt worse. Most of the time, I couldn't even stand up on it long enough to cook dinner. I couldn't get around, and I had a hard time concentrating on anything. The pain meds didn't seem to help. I began to get fevers.

And I lay there, and I thought about having to use Duke's money. It was actually his gambling stake, the reserve he put in my name to keep from his other money or maybe to keep himself from spending everything, I don't know. That's what Claudia, my mother, told me when I came into the money when I was twenty-one. But Claudia gives new meaning to the word bitter, so I never knew whether to believe her or not.

Anyway, I had this little bit of Duke's stash, and I lay there wondering if I would have to use it. I actually wasn't sure. And that was the saddest part of all. I wondered if I would use that money, which I had been saving all my life for a rainy day, for something really important, and I wasn't sure I wanted to use it to save the clinic I had spent, by that time, almost ten of what turned out to be the best years of my life, creating.

And I didn't really have anyone to talk it over with. The one person I would have talked with was the person who was responsible for creating the whole situation, which really infuriated me and still does. So I lay there and stewed in worry. I was alone most of the time, except when friends would come over to cook some food or bring me groceries. My friends were really, really great to me. I knew I was being a bitch most of the time, and I didn't seem to be able to help it. I was crazy with worry. And I didn't know what to do, and I didn't feel like I could bother people by talking about it. God knows, they were doing enough for me already. All I could think was that I was going to have to spend Duke's money, and then I really would have nothing.

That's what's so stupid about all those rumors. So far from taking money from the clinic, I was seriously considering putting quite a bit of money into the clinic. I mean, what else could I do? I thought that's what I was going to have to do.

And you know what? I wasn't sure I could do it. That's the worst thing Annie Bartleby ever did to me. She made me not sure if I wanted to save the clinic which was the only thing I ever really had of my own. I was so angry about it, I couldn't see straight.

I remember Barbara Chadwick came over one afternoon with the books, saying she'd heard I was being morose, and what I really needed was to get to work. So we talked all that afternoon about what the clinic meant to me, and why I was doing it anyway. I thought of people like my attorney, Laura Gilbert, who was a lot on my mind because I looked at her and saw she was my age and had really nice clothes and probably her own personal trainer at her expensive health club and pension funds and a house she owned, and what did I have? A rental house I didn't want to live in anymore, a few extra pounds, and an American car so beat up only a Democrat from a Rust Belt state could have loved it.

Actually, I liked Gilbert at first. I had no idea she would turn out the way she did; she came so well recommended. A friend of Barbara's put me in touch with her and claimed she was the best lesbian personal injury attorney in town, which is pretty scary if you think about what she did to me.

She just didn't want to work very hard, I think. She wanted to make her buck and get out. Production-line law. I can't stand that when anyone does it. I say, an honest day's pay for an honest day's work. "You don't want to work, get a government job," Duke always used to say. But don't act like you deserve to get paid when you don't work. There's too many of us out here working our butts off for no money. Don't act like you can get something for nothing. I just hate that.

Frankly, I don't think she liked what she was doing, but a woman who can't listen any better to her clients than Laura Gilbert did should never have been an attorney in the first place. And she wasn't too bright. I was always having to suggest legal strategies for her to pursue. I liked her before I knew all this. Maybe she was temperamentally unsuited for the job. I don't know. It's all water under the bridge now. She wasn't malicious, and I don't think she was out to get rich—maybe it would have been better if she had been. I might have gotten a bigger settlement.

To be honest with you, I don't know why she took my case. I don't know why she was a lawyer. Maybe you'll find out why when you interview her. She's not an attorney now; I've heard I was her last client. Good thing, too. But I didn't know any of that then, and as I said, she came well recommended. I'll tell you, at the time, I needed recommendations. I couldn't have found my own elbow by myself in those days, my brain was so fried.

I remember when I met her, she was a little standoffish in her manner, a little formal for me, but she seemed concerned I was hurting so much, and I think because of those two things I honestly didn't think about how much she was violating my personal boundaries. When I think about it now, I can't believe I let her so far into my life, but what's done is done. I obviously made a mistake in picking her, a mistake I'll regret the rest of my life, but I was alone, and I did the best I could at the time.

It was a very confusing time for me. Maybe if I'd had a partner or someone to help me—it was just a very rough time. I wasn't really sure I was going to make it for a while. Especially after the first surgery. The pain during surgery was nothing compared to the pain of the infection I got later. The pain just seemed to go on and on, and no matter what meds I took, it didn't get better. I just lay there and brooded. I couldn't see my way clear, and I couldn't see the clinic's future either. I really didn't see how we were going to be able to go on.

It wasn't the medication that was keeping me from getting clear, and I certainly wasn't addicted. God, I don't know where *that* rumor came from. I'm sure it was Annie. I don't need you to confirm that. It's just the kind of thing she would go after.

"No drunk like a reformed drunk," Duke used to say. But part of me, I'll tell you the truth, part of me still can't believe Annie took the money. I still can't believe she would actually take money from the clinic. God knows, I've been wrong before. I remember getting really angry at her one afternoon, and then I realized she wasn't even here for me to yell at, which sent me over the top. Her leaving me and stealing from the clinic at the same time just about did me in. The whole thing made me crazy.

You have to remember, or maybe you can't understand, what it's like to live with pain. You have to try and understand that. I wasn't just physically disabled from the surgery. The pain itself was disabling. And I didn't know how to deal with it then. I mean, I'd been in an accident when I was little that had caused me some amount of pain, but I'd forgotten all that by then, which was probably good. That time involved me being thrown by a car, too, except I started out *in* the car. Actually, it was the accident my father died in.

I was quite young and don't really remember it. And I don't think it had much effect on me, except it made me not able to play pro baseball which was my dream at the time. Of course, there wasn't much reason to play ball if Duke wasn't going to be there to bet on me; the whole thing just got lost. That's all I remember, that and pain. I did remember the pain during the accident when I got hit this time, but it was different.

Or maybe not. I thought it was different, but now today, trying to remember—maybe it wasn't. What I remember most about the days when I was convalescing from Dr. Brice's lack of regard for anything except his wallet, what I mostly remember is just a fog of pain. I would try to work on the books and try to complete a grant proposal or some idea, any fund-raising idea, and I would mostly lie here on the couch in screaming pain.

I had to go to physical therapy three times a week, which was more horrible than I can tell you. First, I had to get down the front stairs, which was always tricky because of the rain. When it was dry, I actually got used to going down on my butt. Of course, when I got to the sidewalk I still couldn't do anything. I couldn't drive. I had to hire a friend of a friend who had AIDS and so was working, on his good days, under the counter, and when he remembered, he would take me. Of course, he didn't always remember, and often he was late—which just drove me wild, as you know—but Fred and I did okay. I had to fire him after a while because he was so undependable, but by that time, I was able to get rides without too much trouble.

At least I didn't have to depend on my friends for all the driving. My friends, particularly Barbara, were so good to me. For a long time, Barbara came over at least one night a week, and we went over the books, looking for money, some money, any money, to keep the clinic going.

I was crazed, and she was patient, and I guess it all worked out. What we did was, when we realized that Annie had taken the operational money, we just decided to take it public, to make a public appeal for money. Honestly, there wasn't anything else we could do. We felt that if women knew the clinic was in trouble and in danger of closing, they would help us. And they did. They really did.

That must have been very gratifying for you. Did you tell anyone that it was Annie who had embezzled the missing funds?

Well, you know, we were never able to prove conclusively that it was her. I mean, we all knew it, but we couldn't prove it in court. And we didn't want the expense or the scandal, well, really more time than anything. We just never wanted the hassle of going to court. We all knew what she had done and that seemed like enough. So we never named her publicly, although anyone who knew anything about the clinic knew. I mean, it was just common knowledge. And by that time, she'd lost all of her bookkeeping clients anyway, and I was glad for that. I don't think she should *ever* have access to anyone's money. I think what she did was wrong, even if she was my lover once, and I hope she's suffered for it, to tell you the truth.

I know that's not very sisterly. But just being a lesbian doesn't make you a saint. It only makes you someone who wants to have sex with other women. It doesn't mean a thing about who you are. I found that out the hard way. To tell you the truth, if it hadn't been for Barbara, I would have lost my faith in the clinic and in myself altogether. Well, Barbara and my partner, Kore.

Kore?

Yes, I know, isn't it a funny name? It's a chosen name from back when she was wild and free and full of the feminist spirit in college. I think it's kind of cute. My lover, Kore Burke. Her given name was Cora, which she hates, thinks it old-fashioned. I like Cora; maybe when she gets older, she'll change it back. Now she wants to be called Burke, and sometimes I remember and sometimes I don't.

Anyway, it was all because of the accident that I met Burke in the first place. She was my home health care attendant. I'd gotten an infection after the first surgery, and they couldn't figure out what it was for a while, and then when they did, I had to have I.V. antibiotics for six weeks. Now that was fun—every two days I got a new needle stick. I had to change my dressings twice a day; this yellow pus stuff kept draining out for months. Oh, that was attractive! I'll tell you, falling in love with someone when they are sticking needles into you or stretching your leg so it doesn't completely atrophy until the tears come or having her change your drain dressing or running the stim machine . . .

The stim machine?

Oh, it's a little electric fryer. What happens is, you get electricity sent to the muscles you have that don't work anymore. You literally get wired. You get some conductor grease put on you and these little electrodes, and then the machine gets turned on and turned up until your teeth rattle and your ears buzz and you scream.

Then, it stops. And you feel better. My one and only experience with S/M, ha! The thing of it is, Burke was so nice to me, even when she was frying me, that I just fell in love with her. Believe me, I knew what it was like to be with someone who wasn't nice to me. Kore could find a vein more gently than anyone, much better than any doctor I ever had stick me.

I hardly knew what to do, Burke was so nice. We've been together ever since. She's really been a great help to me, and she's wiped out any memories of having girlfriends who weren't nice. We never argue. We're best friends. She's great. Stick around, she'll be home soon to fix dinner. She's really the greatest cook. Her mashed potatoes are to die for. I can't complain. Honestly.

But we were not together until later. I mean, from the first, I had my eye on her a little, and she certainly had her eye on me, although I didn't know it, not exactly. But still, mostly, I was alone. My friends were great, but they didn't spend the night after the first week. And I was still not used to being alone.

And out of control. That was the worst thing, and actually, that was the thing that was the most like my first leg injury. The pain was bad, but it wasn't the thing that really got me. What got me was when the meds stopped working, and it was two in the morning, and I couldn't get out of bed. I couldn't get out of bed to go to the bathroom or to get more meds or more water to take the meds or anything. If someone had broken into the house and found me in my bedroom, I wouldn't have been able to get away. I mean, I finally was able to get up and get around at night, but even then, I was terribly afraid of falling, and of course I did fall eventually, but that was later.

What I remember most was having to depend on all these people. People who I didn't really care about, like Fred, and people I did really care about, like Barbara. It's one thing to have a lover care for you when you can't care for yourself; it's another altogether to have to depend on folks you have to ask.

And if you don't think it was hard for me to go to the community and ask for help for the clinic, you're wrong. I never would have done it if it hadn't been for Barbara convincing me it was okay. It's always been difficult for me to ask for help. I don't like to do it, and I don't do it very well.

I know what they say about me out there in the community; I know they call me Mighty Meg, like I was a battleship or something. Personally, I think there is some fat oppression in that nickname. But I don't care what they say, and I don't care if they think I'm the most self-sufficient person on earth. I still need people sometimes; everybody does. But I don't like to ask. I do *not* like to ask.

And I didn't like asking the community for help. I didn't like getting up at fundraisers and asking. It felt like begging to me, and I hated it. I hated that I had been forced into that position, and I hated Annie for doing that to me. I've done some difficult things in my life. Sitting around that conference table at the mediation and being shot at like a fish in a barrel by Brice's goon lawyers was no picnic. Surgery and rehab were so difficult, I wept. Pain can make a person crawl. But there are few things more difficult than explaining to people that you need them to give up their hard-earned dollars to help you because your lover stole money from them, stole from their clinic.

Now that's hard. It was much harder even than going to the city and answering questions about what happened to the budget. That wasn't pleasant, but we got through it, Barbara and I. We just explained what happened and said the book-keeper in question had been fired for incompetence and that we would be able to make it up.

And fortunately, I have to say this, in those days we didn't have any reporters from our own community looking around, trying to bag us, and the big papers couldn't really give a damn what happened in a women's clinic. But you guys, really, I think you should be reporting on real news. I've seen other agencies get bagged by news reports when really all that was going on was an accounting problem.

Do *you* know, for example, how often they change the accounting rules for each grant cycle? Each year they make up new rules. Do you know how hard it is to keep up with all those rules? And some of them are meaningless hoops to jump through, just hoops. And guess who put them there? You reporters. I mean, I like you as a person, but I want you to think about how easily blowing things out of proportion can happen. If you don't know the history of the grant and the history of the accounting guidelines, and know them not only for that year, but for the year the grant started and for the year the clinic started, you have no basis in understanding the story.

Now, this story you say you're writing about me—why don't you guys write real stories more often? Stories about women trying to keep clinics going, about honest folks who are working their hearts out and still not making a decent living, why don't you guys write more stories about that? I know. It's not news. But tell me, what's new about bad news?

Laura

In the weeks following our first meeting, I met with Margaret much more than I ordinarily met with clients. She went into surgery the week after I met her, for reconstruction of her tibial plateau, an open procedure usually requiring at least one night, often two nights in the hospital.

Ah. An open procedure is one where a large skin incision is made, and the surgery is done by opening up to the anatomy, as opposed to a closed procedure, which is done through small incisions, usually involving some kind of remote imaging, like an arthroscopy, for example.

Band-Aid surgery, exactly. Well, Margaret's surgery required considerably more than a band-aid. The surgeon had to open up her knee in order to reconstruct it, building a new bridge using bone grafts. That particular operation is not pretty and can hurt a lot, depending on the patient and their ability to tolerate pain. I assumed Margaret would be no different than most, and so I did not make an appointment to see her again, preferring, as I explained to her during our first meeting, to wait until she called me when she was feeling better. I certainly had enough work to do trying to wrap up my practice.

So I was startled to hear from her the week following her surgery. When my secretary told me she was on the phone, I remember being so surprised, I looked at the date on my calendar and figured back to when I thought she had said she was going in. Before I picked up the phone, I thought to myself, now this is odd, too early, what happened?

"You might as well come over," she shouted into the phone. "Let's get this ball rolling."

Well, I was astonished, to say the least. She did not sound at all like the Margaret Donovan I had met two weeks before and watched from a distance for much longer. This woman sounded coarse and crude, and I was troubled by the slurring in her voice and wondered if her pain meds were being over-done. I probably should have been more cautious about going to her house that afternoon, but frankly, I was worried about her.

I asked if someone were there, hoping someone was looking after her, and trying to get a more accurate picture of what was happening.

"No one's home—just us chickens," she yelled, but it didn't sound like a joke.

I did not particularly want to go over. On the other hand, I told myself, it was late, and she sure sounded like she was in trouble. Maybe if she hadn't been a lesbian, or if I hadn't already accepted her as a client, or if I hadn't been tired, or if I . . .

Well, I have given up trying to count the mistakes I made with Margaret Donovan. Perhaps, as Brenna said, I should have had better boundaries. That's certainly what Audrey kept telling me. "You're an attorney, not a social worker. There is a difference." And of course there was; that was my whole problem with practicing law, if you understand what I mean.

Still, the point is I went, not immediately, but I was able to finish up enough work that I could justify to myself going over, reluctantly, bribing myself over my own misgivings by saying that I would at least have the evening with Brenna, which had been a point of contention for us for a number of years.

We have been together, let me see now, it will be ten years in August, so we would have been together six years at that point. Six years, ten years, they are all tricky years when you are in an active relationship. And believe me, Brenna is the kind of woman who is very actively in her relationships. There is no coasting allowed, and I wouldn't have it any other way, except that it's not my nature really. We were going through a difficult time then, I think mostly because of me. And Brenna was very patient, but she definitely wanted to "connect" as she used to put it, "in a real way and before midnight."

She had a point. I was clear on that. I had been promising her a vacation and had broken the promise three times due to trial dates being moved. And I hadn't been making promises just to her. I had been promising myself a vacation until that day I realized a vacation wasn't going to be enough.

My love for Brenna has never been shaky, and I don't believe her love for me has ever wavered either, but the container we had built around us needed to be overhauled—at least my part did. What I needed was time to sit and think, time to watch the rain come down, time to rethink myself. I wanted to sit in the living room, wrapped up, with Debussy or Ravel on the stereo, listening to Brenna making her sounds as she did her weaving in the next room, and watching the rain over the lake.

Brenna? She calls herself a weaver; I would say an artist. She makes wearable artwork out of woven fabric mostly, although sometimes she has commissions for large wall hangings, which she likes doing, but not too often. She really likes the clothing. She says she likes to think about women wearing it next to their skin. That's my Brenna. We built her a small studio off the kitchen with wonderful windows to the southwest, so she is warm most of the time. Some of my happiest moments have been listening to her sing at her loom as I watched the rain. And I needed that, particularly during that time. I needed that song underneath the quiet of my thoughts to make sense of my life.

It doesn't seem like so much to ask now, but in those days, I was so driven by my work, I think I needed to justify taking the night off by stopping off to see Margaret on my way home.

Well, whatever the reason, when I got there, I was glad I had gone. I don't care what happened later. That afternoon Margaret Donovan was a very sick woman. She was lying on the couch, her dark curls plastered to her face, her eyes bright with fever.

I asked her about pain medication, and she shook her finger at me as though I were a schoolgirl questioning her teacher. I asked about her knee and she began to cry. I asked who was managing her care, and she couldn't tell me.

So I picked up her meds bottle, remembered the surgeon's name, and called for an appointment for her to be seen that afternoon. I had spent too much time in my own father's office not to know that a patient should be seen immediately if a high fever develops in the first few weeks after surgery.

My father was one of those old-fashioned family doctors in Connecticut, where I grew up. My mother was a do-gooder who actually did some good. She ran contraceptives out of New York state for the women who couldn't get them in Connecticut and Rhode Island. She volunteered at Planned Parenthood, kept the bail money for when the Catholic priest complained to the local police and the staff got taken down to the "pokey," as she used to call it. She would go down and bail them out. I used to go with her sometimes. She is an amazing woman. I wish I had half the courage she has.

Of course, I haven't always thought that. When I was a teenager, I thought she was ridiculous and part of me truly believed I was one of my father's patients' foundlings. At the time, I thought my father was a saint. Many summers I worked in his office, helping out while his staff went on their vacations. He was the kind of doc who still made house calls. All I can say now is, it didn't seem so odd to me at the time to make a house call on Margaret myself.

I still don't know if I should have. I could have left her for her friends, but I wasn't sure where they were. There certainly wasn't anyone around when I got there, and it didn't look like anyone had been there all day. I asked her if someone was coming over soon because I didn't want to take her to the doctor. I knew she needed to be seen, but I desperately wanted to go home myself by then. But she either didn't know, or no one was scheduled to come.

Brenna asked me later if I would have made a house call to one of my other clients, and I think probably, if they had been unable to come to me and I liked them, yes, I would have. Then she asked me if I would have taken them to the doctor, and I didn't know. Part of it was that there didn't seem to be anyone there for Margaret, and I couldn't quite believe that. She seemed to know everyone. But I myself had been one of those young women everyone thought was dating, but who stayed home alone on Saturday nights. I kept thinking, wait, this is Margaret Donovan. I couldn't quite put the picture together. It seemed like someone should be coming, but maybe not. What I did know was that she shouldn't go through the night without being checked out.

And so I took her. It wasn't exactly billable hours, and I don't know if I should have gotten so involved, but I can tell you, I know that I couldn't *not* have. If that made me a bad attorney, well, I think we have ample evidence along those lines already, but I'm not sure it answers the question.

Anyway, I took her to the doctor's office, and we waited what seemed to be an interminable time for the doctor to be able to squeeze her in. When the doctor finally was available, she took her in an exam room, tapped her knee, gave her a script for antibiotics, and told her to call tomorrow.

Tapping? Let's see. A non-technical term. Let me see if I can remember. Aspiration. Does that help? No? Well, it involves using a hypodermic needle and a large syringe to remove a sample of fluid for analysis.

Crudely put, as Margaret said when I drove her home, "She stuck a horse needle in my knee and sucked the pus out. It was gross!"

I'm sure it was, but by that time, it was seven p.m., and I was quite certain Margaret was not going to die that night, and I was getting a little irritated. I insisted she call someone when she got home and hoped it wasn't inconsistent that I didn't stay to see if she did. I felt bad, but I went home.

I went home, and I told Brenna what had happened, and she warmed up some red beans she had made me for dinner and listened to me, and I suppose it is not terrible to tell you that I cried that night. I wept for Margaret and her aloneness and her fever and for myself, for all those nights I sat alone and all the nights I was alone when I was with someone, and I watched the rain, and when it was time for bed, I held Brenna as if she were morning mist over the lake, grateful for where I had come home and to whom I had come home and when the holding turned to lovemaking, I cried then, too.

Sometime the next morning, from the office, I called Margaret to see how she was, and thankfully, one of her friends was there, Audrey's friend, Barbara Chadwick, who seemed to have things under control.

Two days later, I got another call from Margaret, only this time, she seemed fine. None of the shouting or bawdiness of the earlier call. She wanted me to come over and start the interrogatories, and I was fine with that. I mean, she seemed like a totally different woman, and I assigned the difference to the infection and her medications.

I needed her to be clear for the interrogatories, at the very least, and to be present, mentally, for the discovery process. Discovery is actually a process not unlike interviewing, except I must ask more precise questions than you do. The idea is to find out exactly what happened and to solicit relevant information: past history, current situation, that sort of thing. Obviously, I needed her to be coherent and able to follow a line of thought.

With that in mind, I set up an appointment with her for the next week. When I got there, to my dismay, the scene was not far off the previous visit, except she was a little more coherent. Again, she was loud and kind of vulgar. It seems they couldn't find out what was causing the infection and kept switching her antibiotics, which kept not working. I left early that night, and we tried again the next week.

When I went the next time, it became obvious that talking with Margaret was always going to be interesting, sometimes abruptly frightening, sometimes transparently sad. Watching a grown woman try to shore up the boundaries of a self that medicine was washing away is a pathetic kind of scene. I felt I was watching her undress in front of me, and I often turned my head away so as not to see.

I didn't think she knew what she was doing most of the time during those visits, but I didn't think she would want me to know that, so I acted as if I didn't. I did pay attention, and maybe I should not have. But if there was anything good about the way I practiced law, it was that I was thorough. I was interested, and I paid attention. I suppose we were not a good match in some ways.

Looking back on it now, I am not sure when it was, during those meetings with Margaret, that she told me about her first injury. But it must have been fairly early on, because even though I had names and approximate dates, it took me a long time to find out that her medical records had been lost in transfer when a new hospital was built. I finally located her doctor, who had been retired from practice for some years, and although he didn't think he had any medical records left on her, he did remember her.

This was great luck, I thought. He was still living near Olympia, where Margaret had been born and raised, only about an hour and a half away from Seattle. I would be able to depose him in an afternoon. I thought it would be easy.

I clearly was not prepared for what I found, even though I had heard some already about Duke and Claudia, Margaret's parents. I guess what I had heard before I went was only enough to make me wonder just who they were and who their child might be.

I knew Margaret had been in an accident with her father, an accident that had caused her enough pain to have night-mares and to switch back and forth from now to then if I got there too early in the afternoon for what she called "our talks." I knew then that pain looked like an old visitor because it had been. But she couldn't tell me exactly what happened.

"That was then and this is now," is all she would say when I pressed her, or if I really pressed her, she would say, "Laura, I simply do not remember and I do not wish to remember." Her eyes would flash and she would fix a look on me that I came to call the Empress Death Stare.

The first time I saw it was during our third meeting. I had asked her about Duke and what had happened to him during the car accident she had been in when she was a child.

It was as though a light switch flipped off inside her. I had clearly said something wrong. The room became very quiet. I was aware of a frozen silence, like ice, and a kind of darkness. I realized, suddenly, we had been sitting there as the sun went down, and there was now only a dim light coming soft as snow from the western windows. For some reason, I was not able to reach up and turn on the lamp beside me. Margaret had turned her face away, focused on the windows, and when she turned back to me, her eyes had become as frozen as the room and as bright as lasers.

I had never been stared at in such a way—as though my body were not made of bone and tendon, but merely a two dimensional representation, and she could laser through me like a video game: I would fall over, dead, and she would be free. There would be nothing there to hurt her anymore.

Which is what I did that day, and often afterward. I learned to apologize and change the subject. More and more, it seemed, there was something, maybe more than one thing, she wanted to conceal more than anything else, certainly more than she wanted to win a lawsuit. I didn't know what lay behind her concealment, but I hoped if I got some information from her doctor about what had happened, I could be perhaps a little less clumsy in my approach.

When I think about it now, I realize I had never seen a client so apparently furious and yet struggling so to be benign at the same time. I suppose it was the nature of my practice that many of my clients were angry, often justifiable given the destabilizing effects of injury. When the time came for settlement, these clients had often worked themselves into a frenzy. It rarely worked the other way. Almost no one ever talked themselves into asking for less money, especially if it meant admitting some small amount of contributory negligence. But few bothered to appear so controlled as Margaret, in control and naíve at the same time.

I am not sure if the nature of the legal process of personal injury suits antagonizes people to the point of not being able to accept any blame for whatever befell them or if people who could not accept any blame in the first place are the kind of people who tend to file personal injury suits. What I had begun to believe was that, in general, personal injury suits were filed by folks who felt the world owed them something and who believed money could make things right and if not right, at least better. Sometimes winning the suit itself would improve their dispositions, but mostly the proof seemed to be in the settlement check.

And I worried about that, but at the time, I told myself that it didn't matter, and anyway, it wasn't up to me to decide who owed whom what and for what reason. It was only my job to get them the most money I could—the litigation process itself would assign and apportion blame, and so I needn't worry about that. Besides, as nearly as I could tell, there had been no contributory negligence on Margaret's part.

That is, until I picked up the police report and went to the scene of the accident. Then, I knew I was going to Olympia for sure. Brice's statement to police included the information that Margaret had turned from locking her car door and walked directly into the path of his car. Not only that she didn't *look*, that she didn't even *turn* in his direction to look, but that she had been putting on her raincoat and so couldn't have *possibly* looked. It seemed deliberate to him. I felt a little chill at the sureness of his statement and couldn't help wondering if there was more to this story than I knew.

Brice said she hadn't just crossed the street. She had, in the vernacular, jaywalked right into him. If this were true, and provable, Margaret's contributory negligence would be at issue, which wasn't a point I felt terribly comfortable contemplating exactly how to explain to Margaret.

I asked her the afternoon before I left for Olympia, "Do you remember if you were crossing the street in the crosswalk?"

She turned to the window, and I did too, momentarily. It had begun to rain. The movement of her hands pulled my eyes away from the window, and I watched her work the quilt, as if she were feeling for something sewn in the lining.

"Laura," she said, very slowly, as she brought her eyes to bear fully on me, "this is Seattle. I know you haven't been here very long, but people in Seattle do *not* jaywalk. It's a matter of civic pride. You are not in Washington, D.C. anymore. Please try to keep that in mind."

I nodded, feeling chastised and meek.

She continued. "Have you been there to look? I *had* to have been in the crosswalk. My car was parked directly in front of the crosswalk. Did you even bother to look?"

"Not from that angle, I don't think. I'll go back and look before we meet next week," I promised.

"Say hello to Dr. Lennox for me, that bastard. Tell him to crank a notch in his traction machine in my memory," she said.

"I will," I promised again and escaped into the rain.

What Gets Left Behind

Margaret

Well, I'm glad you came back. I realized after you left the last time that I had not really given you a good picture of what happened. I was talking with Burke, and she suggested I was shielding Annie, which I certainly am not, so I just wanted you to come back and see if we couldn't set the record straight.

I want to be able to tell you exactly what happened, and I remember it exactly; it's not that I don't, I do. And I'm not shielding Annie. Why would I anyway? Anything that happens to Annie Bartleby is her own damn fault. That isn't it.

It's just that it's hard for me to talk about me and that time. It was a hard time for me. My recovery from the surgery was very, very difficult. My knee got infected about two weeks after the first surgery, and then it took them a long time to figure out what was going on with the infection and how to fix it. They couldn't get rid of it entirely until they took the plate out—

they'd put an L-shaped metal plate in my leg to get my bone to heal in proper alignment—and for some reason I didn't understand, all they could do was suppress the infection until they took the plate out.

That didn't happen until the bone was set, which was about four months later, so for the first six weeks, I had to take I.V. antibiotics and for the rest of the time, I was on oral dosages. Of course, after all that, rehab took a very long time. It took me another four months just to walk again. And through all this, there was the mediation, and all the depositions and interrogations before them, so there was a lot going on for me. It never seemed to end.

I tried really hard to work, to keep going at the clinic, until they could find someone to take the strain off me. It got to the point where things were just being left undone, and the clinic was growing and because I was so sick, I just couldn't keep up. I went on disability long before my settlement hearing because I really couldn't devote the kind of time to the clinic that it needed. I was quite disabled for a very long time, and it was more than two years before I could think about working again.

I've talked to Kore about this, and I think you're right that a lot of people don't understand what happened and why I left the clinic. I started beginning to understand there was a problem there when I began interviewing for job positions a couple of years ago. It seemed like people had some major misconceptions.

Even some people who knew I was badly injured acted like I made so much money off my accident, as one idiot put it, that I didn't need to work anymore. That was so stupid; frankly I just put it out of my mind. These are people who don't seem to be able to understand the concept of "blood money."

I can't begin to explain it and I wouldn't want to try. I don't think the amount I got in settlement is anyone's business, and I think it's a sick curiosity that would even make anyone ask. But let's be clear that it wasn't a fortune, and most of it went to my attorney, the doctors, and the insurance companies anyway. All I can say is that I received less for my injuries, my permanent injuries I might add, than the amount Annie stole from the clinic, and it certainly wasn't enough for me to retire on.

As you said the other week, some people seem to think that I wasn't a good administrator and nearly took the clinic down with me. Well, let them think that, I say. I don't give two shits for someone who could look at what I did with that clinic and come away thinking anything of the kind. I know I lost some job offers because of that rumor, and I just decided then that I didn't want to work with people who couldn't think any clearer than that, so it really didn't affect me.

But as for the rest, Kore says she has also heard some people think I left the clinic because of the embezzlement, but she didn't want to tell me because she knew how upset I would get. Well, I did get upset when you mentioned it the first time you were here, as you know. I'm still upset. It simply isn't true, and it just fries me to hear that. But there is no way to stop a lie like that. The woman who is spreading the lies would just make up another lie. I guess she thinks if she tells a big enough lie, someone will believe her. And I guess maybe she's right. So was Hitler. I suppose that puts Annie in good company.

I would like to say, for the record, that I had nothing to do with the embezzlement, except to get the clinic on a good footing after it was discovered. Once things were secure, I stopped working part-time and went on long-term disability, which happened right after my fall. The truth is, I should have left much, much sooner. I should have left once the infection was discovered because truthfully, it was such an effort to carry on with my work, I wasn't putting enough energy into getting well—and so I wasn't.

Not that I could get anyone to pay attention to how I was feeling then. All they seemed to think was that I was guzzling pain meds like an addict. Like I was taking so many pills because I liked it. Like I liked lying there in screaming pain and so I was causing the pain, so I could get more meds. Insanity. Just insanity.

I should have forced that goddamn doctor to listen to me. That's another thing. Write this down. If people think they are going to get a good doctor just because she's a lesbian, they need to think that through again. This woman was so set against giving out pain medication that she accused me of becoming addicted. Damn right I was getting addicted. My entire knee pussed out two weeks after the operation. I'm lucky I didn't die. These rabid p.c. recovery people have changed the climate so much, I couldn't even get enough medicine to be able to function. I was in danger of dying from infection, and all they could say was, well, you won't die an addict. I can't tell you how reassuring I found that.

Well, I don't know how it got infected, to tell you the truth. The doctor acted like I did it on purpose, just to get attention. Just so I could come in to see her. I suppose I had nothing better to do. "Drama queen," I heard one of the office staff call me one day. They think you can't hear them when they're talking in the hall. Or maybe they just don't give a damn if you do. God, I hated that office by the end.

When they finally decided what the problem was, by which time I had been forced to take every kind of antibiotic available, they told me it was some kind of mutated version of an ordinary staph infection, and I wasn't responding very well to the antibiotics because I'd had so many when I was young. Well, I'm not at all sure I believe that. If I hadn't needed that doctor to make my case in the personal injury suit, I never would have continued with her. And I can tell you, I haven't seen her or her sorry little office staff once, not once, since I got my settlement. I go to my chiropractor now for pain management, and we do at least as well as I ever did with mainstream medicine.

I'm telling you, I was in that doctor's office twice a week for six weeks for a dressing change. I'd go on the days I didn't go to physical therapy. If I didn't see Kore in between visits, I'd end up screaming.

The dressing changes weren't so bad in the hospital. Well, they did have to take me back to the hospital after the infection was discovered, or maybe they finally believed that there was something else wrong with me, is more like it. They drained the pus out and don't ask me about it because I don't want to go into it. Let's just leave it that they got almost two full cups, by the time they were done. Then they washed the wound, lavage they call it, and then—this is the really gross part—they packed the wound with gauze and left it open so the dressing changes would be easier.

Well, easier for them. Why is it in medicine everything is for the ease of the doctor? I mean, I could see it every time she reached down there and pulled the gauze out. It was disgusting. And it hurt. It hurt a lot. For a long time, when they couldn't get the right antibiotic in me, I thought I was going to die. Did they care about that? No. And when a culture finally showed it was some mutant staph, that was still my fault, they seemed to think, because I'd had to have so many antibiotics after my first accident, when I was thrown from a car into a ravine.

No, I don't want to talk about it.

Anyway, the point is, it took my doctor a really long time to get me on the right medicine. And for those first two weeks, it was hell. I had temperatures of 104 every night. I really did think I was going to die. And I don't remember much of it, frankly. Except sweating, I remember that, sweating and being unable to find a dry spot in my bed that I could move to without moving my leg. I could hardly breathe, the pain was so bad.

I finally got home health care about that time, not without an incredible struggle from the insurance company. Like I didn't need it, like it was my idea of a good time, thank you very much. God, of all people, the insurance company should have had some idea of the kind of pain I was in, my bills were high enough.

One good thing was when Kore was assigned to me. I knew the woman who ran the home health agency, so I was able to pull a few strings and get a lesbian sent out to help me, but I never dreamed I'd be so lucky as to get Kore.

I had never understood before how men could fall in love with their nurses, but for the first time, I was able to appreciate Hemingway, believe me. God, I was so sick before she came to take care of me.

Anyway that's what happened. If you want to know what day we discovered the embezzlement, you have to understand nothing happened on any one day during that time, and now you know why. I don't remember much of what happened during those weeks. All I know is, there were no operational funds left for the clinic to run on; there were only grant funds for specific services.

Let me see if I can try to explain. We did have some, not many, but some, clients who actually had private insurance. I am not sure why they came to the clinic, but I'm sure they were mostly lesbians—many who, as a group, would apparently do anything to avoid seeing a regular doctor, and honestly, I now agree. We don't trust doctors, with good reason.

But, the doc at the clinic at that time was a politically radical doctor who was open to alternative treatments, which didn't sit very well with the licensing board or the state, but we didn't care. We thought she was great. And she was. And lots of lesbians began coming to the clinic for that reason and also many had already come because we always used nurse practitioners rather than M.D.'s anyway. So we did have some clients for whom we could actually bill private insurance.

Now Annie Bartleby handled all that. Once I showed her what an HICFA 500 form was, she was off and running. For years, I didn't even think about that part of the budget. Once a month, we would go over the aged-accounts sheet so I could present the board with an accurate statement of fiscal health, but other than that . . .

Okay, an HICFA 500 form is, or was before on-line billing, the universal billing form. If you've ever filed a claim form with your insurance carrier, you've seen one; you just didn't know it was called that. An aged-accounts listing is the other side of the billing. That list tells you what accounts have not been paid and for how long. There is usually about a three-month lag time between when bills are sent and when they get paid by the insurance company. So, for example, when Jane Smith's account is sixty days overdue, we get Dido, our receptionist, to call Jane's insurance company and find out where the money is.

Annie always made the personal collection calls to patients who directly owed us money, when their insurance had paid, but they hadn't paid their co-payment. Those calls were distasteful to me; I thought we should just let them go and write the numbers off the books. I really believe healthcare should be free to those who need it. On the other hand, we needed that money to run the clinic, so Annie took care of all that.

Annie would do those calls on the weekends or after dinner, when I had to be at the clinic to work on other problems. There were always problems. It's true that I didn't follow the aged-accounts as closely as I should have. I didn't know that an account 120 days overdue has less than thirty percent chance of collection; I just didn't know that then. And when Annie left, I was honestly too overwhelmed to watch what was happening with the aged-accounts. I didn't know who paid and who didn't and truthfully, I didn't even notice I wasn't getting the reports anymore, and I wouldn't have known where to look to find them anyway.

So, I wasn't tracking the money, and that was my fault. I take full responsibility for that. But that was only one problem. The other problem was that Annie was the only one to enter all the charges into the computer, and she was the only one who knew how. There was a time when I knew, but I had forgotten it by the time she left.

Now maybe you can make a case for that being my fault, too, but the way the clinic was set up, and as short on staff as we always had to run because of inadequate funding, it didn't seem like such a bad idea to have my partner helping us out as a volunteer. I now understand that to have the same person entering charges and entering payments is to invite trouble. It never, never occurred to me that *my partner* would rip us off. Would it occur to you?

Well, I never dreamed she would do that. But that's what she did; she ripped us all off, and I don't care who knows it. I lay there, night after night, dripping sweat, feverish, out of my mind. I couldn't remember who or where I was for hours, and then when I came to, I couldn't remember if I had paid the house rent, and I wasn't sure if I had remembered to pay the rent on the clinic, and I would just lose it. And no one, no one ever punished Annie Bartleby for any of that. I wouldn't have cared if she had gone to jail. Frankly, jail is the least of what I think she deserved.

Exactly what Barbara and I discovered was that there was almost nothing in the aged-accounts to support the clinic. There was no money coming in, and the aged-accounts had been milked dry. Annie must have taken it all with her when she left because it sure wasn't there when we looked later. There were no operational funds to run the clinic on, because that money came out of the private billings, do you understand? When Barbara was finally able to get an aged-accounts report out of the computer, and I was finally able to clear my head long enough to go over it with her, there was no money left to get.

We had to go to the board with it. I'll never forget sitting there, my leg propped up on a chair, so feverish I thought I'd float out of the room, having to tell those ten board members, most of whom were new, that the clinic was broke. I remember

Barbara looked around the room, asking for suggestions, and only Lucky Howell, a new board member who was in private practice as a physical therapist, had the least idea what we were talking about.

I remember looking at her and thinking, God, can't somebody fix this? I remember being so sick I watched Lucky talk, and her words seemed to me to separate from her mouth, as though she were a cartoon or talking in slow motion. And all she asked was if we had a billing clerk now, as if we hadn't already taken care of that as soon as Annie left, as if we hadn't immediately begun interviewing people. I remember then Lucky said, she'd be happy to come in and go over the billing process with me which made me furious; she acted as though we didn't know what we were doing. Nothing like a new board member to come in and act like they had all the answers. I hated that.

But again, I was glad Barbara was there, because she handled Lucky: agreed to whatever she wanted, so as to not antagonize her, and then got down to the point of the meeting, which was, if that board couldn't come up with any solutions, we were going to have to either expand the board, because we needed help, or close the clinic.

We were already in the process of expanding the board and had been, since Barbara had pointed out how much we needed the help, so it wasn't much of a stretch for anybody. We did expand the board to twenty, and we did get help, but I don't remember much of that. I remember Lucky's bright red shirt, how it floated in front of my eyes like my favorite earrings, but that's about it.

Now do you understand? I was so sick I couldn't run the clinic. I was doing my best, but I couldn't keep up. I couldn't keep a grip on the board, and truthfully, I couldn't keep a grip on myself. Laura was coming by every week, trying to get me ready for the depositions from Brice's scum lawyers, who had apparently been told that *I* had walked into Brice's car, and they were thinking about suing *me* for counter-damages.

Now, I want you to think about this. A man hits me with his car, and I have to pay him. I was so angry the first time Laura told me I could have spit nails. I mean, I was *there*. I know what happened. If you want to know what really happened, you ask someone who was there, just like you are doing with me, right?

Finally, after I pleaded with her, Laura went out and tried and tried to find someone who saw the accident. She had signs put up. She advertised. Nothing. I couldn't believe it; I know someone saw that accident because I saw them crowded around me afterward. But no one would come forward. And so, I guess Dr. Brice felt he could say whatever he wanted, he could make up some story, some fantasy, some way to make a buck off his own negligence. Fucking doctors.

I lay there in bed, and I couldn't move and half the time I couldn't think. But when I could, I assigned both Brice and Annie Bartleby special adjoining rooms in hell. They deserved it. And all the while, in the middle of the night when I was alone and awake, of course . . . I was always awake; I don't think I slept one entire, completely whole night from the time of the accident until about two years later. Ever since I got hit, I've had terrible sleep disturbance. When I got the settlement, I went to UW for a work-up at the sleep clinic, but all they could tell me was that it wasn't physical.

Well, bullshit. More help from the medical profession. I'd like to see some of those doctors have an open wound in their knee that won't scar for six months, and see if it doesn't keep them awake at night, especially if they don't know where their next meal is coming from.

Anyway, the point I'm trying to make is that I'm not sure how Annie Bartleby stole from the clinic. We think she was billing under the clinic name and posting the checks to a separate bank account, meanwhile backing charges out of the computer after the bill went out, so the charge never showed up on the monthly print-outs or the aged-accounts. What? Well, some people who wanted to be kinder than I was called it "misappropriation of funds." But believe me, it was stealing. Pure and simple.

I don't really know how she did it. All I know is that for almost two years in a row, for almost twenty-four months, we had an average monthly income from private insurance company reimbursements for goods and services of almost twenty thousand dollars. That's how we ran the clinic. And then, within one month of Annie's leaving, that started to drop by about five thousand a month until there was nothing, which no one noticed until Barbara got a hold of it. The only way to explain it is that the checks were going elsewhere.

Maybe you can tell me where that money went. My estimate is that Annie took us for more than fifty thousand dollars, at least. That's a lot of money, to me. I wish I'd gotten that in my settlement. And it was a lot of money to the clinic. It's enough to buy a person a florist business, if someone is so inclined. And it's enough to kill a clinic, if someone was so inclined. If someone really wanted to hurt a person who really loved the clinic, wouldn't they try to get back at the person by killing what they loved most?

That's my personal opinion, and I don't care if you print it. I think it's possible, and I think it's probable, and I think that's what Annie did. I don't think she needed fifty thousand dollars to move, and I don't think she could have spent that much on her new lover, even if the lover had no politics at all and wanted Annie to buy her a new home on Vashon. I just don't think Annie did it for the money. She never cared that much about money anyway. Why else would she have taken it? You ask her that, will you?

I think she did it to hurt me. And she did. I'm not going to lie to you about that. She hurt me, and I haven't forgotten it. I don't think about it at all now, and actually I don't much care anymore, except for the clinic. But I wouldn't cross the street to help her, and I will not shield her from you; I will not shield her at all.

Laura

It was raining the day I drove down to Olympia, which is not out of the ordinary in Seattle. It seems like it rains a little bit almost every day here, but I'm sure that's not true. Still, as Margaret had informed me frostily one day when I mentioned the weather to her, it rains twice as much in Olympia as it does in Seattle, and that *is* saying something. It wasn't much rain, but it was rain.

Seattle to Tacoma felt like one long suburban strip mall, and it wasn't until I hit the Nisqually Delta that I felt like I had finally traveled out of urban sprawl and gotten to a different place than America-in-the-late-twentieth-century where even the topography has been overwhelmed by the use of architectural design in the service of commerce. We are so separated from the physical place upon which the buildings are located and through which we must make our way that I wonder how we *can* make our way. I could have been anywhere in America, but if all the places looked the same, where was home? I wondered how Margaret felt traveling down this stretch of road, and I wondered if she came this way, if she ever came home.

I wasn't actually going to Olympia, but a little farther on to Shelton, where Dr. Lennox had retired. I had made an appointment to talk with him in the morning because I wanted to see what he remembered, and then I would prepare him for the deposition I had scheduled for that afternoon.

I liked him very much over the phone. "Of course," he remembered Margaret. "Duke's little girl," he called her. "Terrible tragedy." Most of his records had been destroyed or sent to the hospital when he retired, but he'd see if he had anything left. He said he'd be glad to help in any way he could. "Come by and talk any time." He sounded like my dad. Not enough to do in his retirement after so many years of being too busy to wind his watch.

The countryside unfolded under the steady rhythm of my windshield wipers set on the slowest speed. Nisqually was undeveloped and beautiful; Olympia was like Tacoma without the sulfur smell from the paper mills. But it was quite small for a state capital, I thought, and I was soon on the other side, headed up to Shelton.

And here, on Highway 101 North, I finally drove into the past. I ended up on a state road that headed north to the temperate rainforest of the Olympic Peninsula, as densely dark as a mossy tomb, gray and black with decay and rot from the winter rain. That is to say, what was left of the forests from the old growth that had been clear-cut from the Cascades west to the coast and east past the Rockies.

There were no fast food chains here, just lumber trucks and pickups. Some of the forests I passed wore signs trumpeting replanting from clear-cut. What was there now only gave an indication of what had been there before: fir and spruce reaching two hundred feet into the overcast sky, hemlock and cedar filling in below.

The sky was covered by a ceiling of gunmetal gray, a dark and heavy gray, forced downward, a gray that could pin a person directly to the earth without the possibility of flight. The dark trees crowded the road, crowded the hills, could have crowded a small person out, could have crushed her. Between the clouds bearing down and the trees reaching up, there wasn't much room. And then there was the rain. Always the rain.

It was a softer rain than Seattle, and not at all like back home where the rain came in like a scythe from the north. Here it seemed pervasive and formless, as cold as winter, but without an edge or an end. It was said true Washingtonians ignored the weather, but that has always seemed to me more like a fish ignoring water. The rain was in the air, even when nothing was falling to earth, rain was being cast back into the air in smells and mold. I did not see how things ever dried out and wondered what could grow here. Then, abruptly cresting a rise, I was in Shelton.

There was, of course, the obligatory lumber mill at the end of town and a train whistle blowing mournfully. There wasn't much to the town, not more than ten blocks square, and Dr. Lennox's house was not hard to find; his yard was as tidy as his boredom, I suspected.

He came to the door himself, looking rather like a bear, somewhat disheveled, but warm. He had dressed for me, though. I felt pretty sure he did not ordinarily wear such a nice sweater vest or tie a four-in-hand every day. Some part of me was touched by his effort. He apologized for not having coffee ready. His wife had gone to the hospital that morning to do her volunteer work, which seemed to please him. We settled in his study—him in a chair at his desk and me in an old, lumpy couch; he lit a pipe.

"Duke's little girl. What a tragedy," he said again. "The whole thing was in all the papers at the time, Duke being the kind of man who cut quite a swath. Though he moved in very different circles at different times, they all seemed to love him.

"The accident was a terrible thing. Terrible thing," he shook his head and puffed vigorously on his pipe for a moment or two. "The newspaper hounds kept writing articles about 'poor little Margaret,' like she was a poster girl or something." It worried him. "And the thing of it was, sure, she was in the hospital for a long time. But it was her daddy being gone more than her injuries—he was such a good man. Well. I mean, he did have a gambling problem, of course. And he probably did drink a little too much . . .

"And the mother," smoke swirled around his head, "well,

she had problems of her own. I mean, she came to visit Margaret and all that, but . . . Maybe not quite as often as Margaret wanted. Or me, for that matter. But, you know, she was dealing with her loss, too. Margaret was in the hospital for over two months. And then, well, there was no insurance money. Duke had," he stopped to cough a minute, "he'd cashed the insurance in. For gambling debts, I suppose. So . . ."

He poked in the bowl of his pipe and puffed some more. "In traction. Margaret was. In traction for over two months. Her daddy gone. Her mommy distracted. Lots of pain. It was a terrible thing in those days, trying to straighten out the leg as it healed. Pain to keep from creating more pain. We had such limited tools. Not like today. Every time I had to order a new degree of weight," his eyes crinkled and almost seemed to flinch, "I had to steel myself against her wan face and dark-ringed eyes."

Dr. Lennox swiveled his chair to look out the window. "See that rose?" He pointed to a vigorously blooming peace rose. "Duke gave me that. He didn't always pay in cash." Lennox laughed and looked over the top of his glasses at me. "Those union men. Good boys, most of 'em. Wouldn't give two bits for the bosses or the union leadership. But the boys? The rank and file? Taken care of many a logger for free," he nodded. "Still do. Why not? They deserve it." He looked at the rose for a long time.

I withheld prompting him as long as I could, but finally knew I had to push him. "Doctor? The records, do you remember exactly what happened to Margaret's left leg?"

He turned back to me, looking surprised. "Of course, young lady. You think I'm an old man reminiscing. Well, I am, I guess. But I know we have business to do." He smiled. "Let's get the ball rolling, as Duke used to say."

There had been a car crash. Margaret and Duke had apparently been riding around in his new convertible with the top down, even though it was raining. "But it was a Godsend for Margaret, that top being down. She was thrown clear of the wreck, which probably saved her life. The car exploded, tearing Duke's body apart, burning beyond recognition whatever was left."

"Margaret saw the car explode?" I asked. "She saw her father being blown to smithereens?"

He shook his head firmly. "I doubt it. She was unconscious when they brought her in. She never seemed to remember anything about the accident. Her thigh bone was broken clear in two." He'd come to the hospital as soon as he heard. "Got one of the orthopods from UW to come down, take a look, there just wasn't much they could do. It healed well, a tiniest bit shorter than her other leg, even though we'd done our best to pull it out. Maybe I should have been harder on her, but it was nothing that should be affecting her now."

He'd wanted to follow up with her longer. "I urged her to be more active. And I refused to give her those diet pills her mother tried to get for her. Well, there were some disagreements there. Claudia, well. Claudia was small and slender. A different physique altogether than her daughter who was a bit raw-boned, more like her father's side. And of course, when the widow remarried Fullman, well, I didn't see Margaret anymore."

"Of course?"

"Well, Fullman was a doctor himself. And he had his own doctors. I did see her out at the club, though, as she got older. She was an incredible golfer. What a swing! She could drive better than any of the boys her age. Was bigger than most of them, too. Duke would have been so proud. Probably would have been some of the only bets he would have collected on."

"What actually caused the accident?"

Dr. Lennox swung his chair around toward the window once more and was silent for so long that I thought I'd have to prod him again; then suddenly he said, "No one really ever knew. It was raining . . . but then it's almost always raining."

He'd turned back toward me, and we smiled at one another. He shrugged. "Duke had been drinking. That was certain. He'd been seen, with little Margaret in tow. But then, she usually was with him. She adored her father, just adored him. And he her, as well. Sometimes, it seemed like she was more his wife than daughter."

He shook his head roughly. "Old man," he seemed to say to himself. "Anyway, you'd have to know Duke. That man could have charmed the socks off a queen. No lie! And he did, when he married Claudia Peele. None of us could figure that one out. Maybe she believed he'd settle down after the war and do something with his law degree. Or maybe he just swept her off her feet.

"Not that he ever did. Use his law degree, I mean. Oh, he had offers, plenty of them, I heard. He came home a war hero in that bomber jacket, looking for something. Plenty of the old firms wanted him—young, charismatic, fierce. Whatever he was looking for, he didn't find it in a law office. Or at home, I suspect."

He fiddled with his pipe once again, and I kept the silence with him.

"He was not the kind of man to live long. But while he was here—men, women, kids—hey all loved him. I never really expected him to come back in one piece from the war. Oh, he was a rake. But he loved his little girl, I can tell you that. The only time I saw him not moving in three directions at once was when he was with her.

"And losing him cost her more than all the bones she broke in that little body of hers. That broken heart wasn't ever mended, I don't think. I used to watch her at the Sunday buffet out at the club, and I would turn to Lillian, my wife, and I would say, 'She's just eating her heart out.' Lillian would pat my hand and say, 'Jack, you can't heal every part,' and I knew she was right, but I wished I had been able to do better by Duke's little girl."

I sat on the old couch and watched him watch the birds going after the worms turned up in the garden by the rain. I remember thinking, well, if I can get to a phone, I can at least cancel the deposition. No need for that unless opposing counsel insisted on it, in which case it would be their nickel. And I also remember wanting to take his hand and pat it the way he said his wife did, certainly the way my own mother did, and tell him that Margaret had turned out okay, which is what I did, I guess. He wanted to know how she was, and I told him she was a great success, that she had built a wonderful clinic that offered health care to any woman who needed it.

"You've done my heart a world of good today," he said finally, after clearing his throat and taking a big white cotton handkerchief out of his pocket to clean off his glasses. He slowly wiped them clean, put them back on, and looked directly at me. "I'd been worried about that girl for a long time. Ever since Duke left her behind."

Less than an hour later, I was winding my way back down to Olympia, headed to the library. I still had half a day. I couldn't bring myself to stay for lunch with Lennox, though he'd offered. I pleaded work. Used his phone. Looked important. But I suppose in a way, I *was* going back to work. I wanted to see those newspaper articles. I wanted to see everything.

I drove back into town with my window down, feeling the wet air around me like a compression chamber. In downtown Olympia, where I hoped to find a library, there was still the smell of forest mildew, but also the fish-salt smell of ocean water from the many-fingered cup of the base of the Puget Sound where ocean water meets freshwater in the estuary at Nisqually, and at Capital Lake just below what must have been, in Margaret's childhood, a disintegrating downtown. There was still, downtown near the foot of Capital Way, the clean smell of fresh-cut lumber.

As I drove back through town, I could see the direction of

Olympian development had been away from downtown, out to the suburbs built into what used to be called Black Hills. That's where the hospital had moved to, where the lost records would not be. The old hospital, where Margaret had spent so much time, had been destroyed to make room for change, the same change that brought men from all over America to cut the forest down, the forests that called to them with the smell of manly work and hard cash.

The forests would not have been entirely gone during Margaret's youth, but the timber industry was even then in decline. It had always been a hard way to make a living, for both the loggers and the mill owners. Accidents were common. The work was badly paid, the profit margins small, and everybody wanted a piece of the action because there was so little else. But rain. There was always the rain.

None of this was hard for me to imagine, even sitting in the sterile, modern, county library, watching the years slide by under the magnified gaze of the microfilm machine, while the rain slid down the floor-to-ceiling plate glass windows.

Most of Olympia's mills moved away before the Second World War. The knitting mill, the brewery, the working wharves down at Perceival's Landing, and the steamships that had docked there for fifty years, all had vanished, taking with them the robust, hopeful, frontier-town mentality and the town establishments that served that mentality, that dream.

The dream hadn't died here, only moved north, as the timber gave way to airplanes in south Seattle. The timber industry was not the first, only a local variant for those men and women anyway, for that dream of working their sweat and blood together in the rain long enough to make it, make enough. Hell, they deserved it. This was America, after all, and the Great Northwest, the end of the line. There would be enough for everyone, for anyone who just worked hard enough.

Enough money for a man without a family anyway, all that uneasy money that could never buy enough even if you spent it on a sure thing in Spar's back room, even if you spent it on a pretty young girl just off the train from Seattle who the bell boy at the Olympian Hotel swore was a friend of his sister's, even if you saved it all and gave it to the church—that money and that mentality was never enough.

Oh, the dream of salvation, the dream of rescue or riches, only the names changed. And it hadn't completely left Olympia, maybe it never completely leaves any of us, we who need to dream to keep on going. Maybe we only reform those dreams, move, revise, spruce up, or paint over. Maybe that's all my law practice had ever been—for my clients and for me.

The dream had certainly been spruced up at Spar's, the restaurant which had apparently been Duke's hang-out. The day after the accident, there was a front page picture of Duke and Margaret—two dark, curly heads together, grinning over a newspaper and a plate of eggs from some breakfast at Spar's. "Crash kills father, little girl hospitalized."

A convertible. Early evening. He had taken her to a Tacoma Clippers baseball game that afternoon. He had been seen drinking. The mother had been at home, waiting. There was a dance at the country club. He was late, but then he always was. The mother was waiting and watching from the window of the living room in the little bungalow they'd bought after the war, the little bungalow he'd promised would be replaced by a suburban house, but never was. He honked the horn; she came out to be picked up; he was late. He was going too fast. It was raining. The car began to spin on the ninety-degree turn at the end of the street and seemed to skid off the road into thin air, then flipped, landing upside down in the Murphy's front yard, teetering for a second or two before exploding.

Margaret was thrown from the car, left femur broken in two, with one end sticking out of her skin and her pants. Claudia did not see this because she ran back in the house, screaming into the phone for the ambulance.

"Little Girl Improving." Two months later: "Donovan Girl to Be Released Today." There is ten-year-old Margaret, looking like Dr. Lennox's "poster child," except she's not smiling. She is definitely not smiling. Claudia is smiling bravely. She has hope, or at least wants us to believe that she does, and that she is a good mother, even though she was not in the car.

I looked up from the papers and saw that it had gotten late. That smile, that hope. It wasn't hard for me to imagine, even though my people had not been hopeful like that for years. New Englanders to the core, they didn't have to worry about hope. They took the long view. Things would work out. We just had to keep working at them. We, of course, could afford to wait. We didn't need hope. We had history. In my mind, I saw my mother at the breakfast table, my father at dinner, both smiling brightly. "Of course, darling. It just might take a little longer, but you'll get there."

I believed it. Spent my whole life living it. My people didn't need to be hopeful. They were where their families had always been. Doctors, lawyers, understated, active. And they gave me a place from which to view the world that I came to realize had nothing to do with most peoples' lives.

Brenna's family, for example—the newly middle class. She had the courage to fight them, to hurl herself away from their terror. For the newly middle class is not hopeful, only fearful of losing what they have so recently acquired, only terrified of losing it again, of falling back, in the way Claudia's tight smile, velvet grasp on Roger Fullman's arm in the picture two years later, shouted terror. I thought of Brenna's mother in the pictures from home, those pictures sent to try to call her home every holiday, never understanding Brenna had moved to an entirely different world for a reason.

Claudia had married an attorney the first time. This seemed to have been a slight miscalculation. I flipped back, took one more look at the picture of Duke back from the war, wavy haired, big dark-eyed sweetheart, smiling. He would have made anyone hopeful, even Claudia, especially Margaret. What happens to any of us, after all, when we don't have a roof over our heads or when our souls are galvanized in the fear of that loss?

I walked outside then, stepping around my car, too much inside me to go back home just yet. The smell of fresh-stripped lumber was still full in the air, the way it must have been all of Margaret's early years, even though all that was left now were the logging trucks and the boomers out on the water, rafting the logs for delivery at Port Angeles. All that was left was the dream of more.

And that had been there all along. As much as the rain. Duke's death didn't stop that. By the sixties, everything and nothing had changed. Boeing had made a huge success of itself further north. All the bright boys left town, if they could. Successful families moved from the expansive but old-fashioned Craftsman's bungalows at the center of town, where Margaret was born, out to the new houses in the suburbs—those new houses in old styles, badly done, like the neoclassic Georgian into which Claudia and Margaret moved when Claudia married Dr. Roger Fullman.

A picture in the society pages: Dr. and Mrs. Roger Fullman. Margaret was in the picture, a little to one side. Dark, Irish, sullen, large Margaret. A perfect new house, a perfect new husband, a perfect new life? How could Duke's daughter have fit in, what could she have been to a perfect lady like her mother? A petite blond with delicate features, flawlessly coiffed hair, the perfectly manicured and polished nails placed so gently on her perfect new husband's sleeve, only slightly turned to display the size and dazzle of the diamond. I imagined Margaret's nails to be chewed to the nub, ragged and uneven.

But then I thought of that picture of Duke just after the war. Big and rugged, a mischievous grin matching the glint in his eyes, exuding excitement, sexuality. And a pretty, young

Claudia—so in love, so hopeful. And how that love and hope dwindled as she spent the next years waiting for Duke to return, wasting her hope on paychecks squandered on gambling or booze. Or women? Watching her hope get felled like the great forests around her. I had to ask myself, was it fair to judge Claudia for marrying a man like Roger Fullman? An attempt to restore hope through security, a security that must have been entirely missing in her marriage to Duke. What was the cost? To her? To Duke's daughter?

With a mother and stepfather like Claudia and Roger, Margaret's athleticism took on new meaning. A perfect mother who had saved her life from an imperfect father, who had clearly adored her and nearly killed her. Duke's shady activities were so well known and well accepted that the paper felt comfortable mentioning them in the obituary.

That mention must have driven Claudia wild. She must have felt much better standing in front of Roger Fullman's dream house, a house almost clear-cut itself out of the lush vegetation surrounding the country club suburb. A house that looked as dark inside as the forest was behind the house, dense and forbidding, when I drove past it on my way out of town that night.

That house—away from downtown and the gambling, the shouts and the fights, the excitement in the air, the get-rich-quick, the vice, saloons, and Chinatown—was in the opposite direction of Duke's life. And Margaret's life with him. It all must have vanished for her like a ghost, like he did that one night, suddenly, without warning. How would a child have survived that? How *could* a child have survived that?

Two pages away from the dream house picture, I noticed a small story on the continuing library renovation and realized then that Margaret had been left with nothing, nothing to bring her home. The library where she had lived when she was younger, when Duke dropped her off and proceeded down to Spar's back room or put in an hour or two at his tiny office in the Security Building, that library was gone. She must have had nothing left when he died except her feelings. And where were they now? Was only the anger left?

I walked the four short blocks from the new library, past the old library—the one built with Carnegie money, the one Margaret loved, the one with the books she gave as her only request ("Hospitalized Girl Pleads for More Books")—past the boarded-up Olympian Hotel, down to the Security Building. Spar's was just around the corner.

It was past five then, and I stood in the lobby of the Security Building, watching the office workers go home for the day. Margaret must have loved this place, I thought: the plaster flowers on the lobby ceiling, the smooth marble floors in three colors she could have skated on if she wore her mary-janes and Duke was taking her to the China Clipper for lunch, the mail chute she could listen to and watch the letters whizzing by. I put my cheek against the glass chute, and it was not hard to imagine. It was not hard to imagine at all, but I wondered where it had all gone inside her. And I grew cold then, too, before I walked back out into the rain.

The Real
Issues

Margaret

No, don't apologize; I've gotten used to you being late.
Besides, the people here know me, and I've just been sitting,
reading my book, and eating these fabulous chips. Sit down.
Have some.

I'm glad you've decided to expand the length of your
article. And I'm really glad someone finally wants to talk about
real issues, because women's health care is a real issue if you
care about women at all.

There's been all this talk, and money I might add, energy
and focus, that's really the word I want to say, focus, on men's
health and health care for men. And I don't mean just AIDS.
That's fine and, of course, women get AIDS too, although we
don't get the funding for it. But women don't get the funding for
anything, for any of our health concerns. They don't even
include women in the epidemiologic studies to see what we

might need in the way of funding. It's insane, and it's been going on a long, long time.

Well, it's patriarchy, I guess, is really what it is, and that *is* insane. Should I get us some more chips and salsa?

How did I get into this? Well, I've always been kind of involved in health care delivery, although it wasn't called that. My father, my real father, Duke Donovan, was a lobbyist for organized labor at the Washington State Legislature until he died, working for years on the issue of universal health care. And that was a long, long time ago.

I can remember going to baseball games with him when I was a kid and watching him pat guys on the back. Then he would come back to our seats, with a soda or ice cream or whatever for me, and he'd sit down and he'd say, "No left leg, logger" or "Lost his right hand on the rig." Like that. But it was always what injury, then how and what industry they worked in.

The loggers' injuries were terrible. Not that the fishermen's were much better, but they were not worse. The loggers were the worst I saw as a child. And, boy, this will tell you something. The guys who owned the mills, they said they were in "forestry" or they would say the "timber industry." The guys who actually did the work, oh, they were just loggers. They didn't work in an "industry." They worked in the mud. The work was dirty and cold and miserable. Very early, like in 1915, the men in the "timber industry" pushed the first workers' compensation bill through the legislature—the first in the country. But by 1930, the whole thing was as toothless as an old dog, and it hadn't had many teeth to start with. They had only written the law because of the Wobblies anyway, because the Wobblies had been so successful organizing the loggers they had practically started a class war here in Washington. Everyone knew that.

I remember Duke telling me about the guy who owned a big mill up in Shelton. One of his loggers lost both his legs in a boom smash-up, and he was convalescing in the company hospital. Day after day, he watched the mill owner go to and from work, watched him walk right past his hospital window. Now this was a guy who was only in his twenties, and he knew he never would have a way to support his family again, no way to make a living and the company wouldn't give him a dime. Said whatever he got from the state was what he got. Well, fine. So one day this guy, the one without the legs, he goes and orders a shotgun, mail order. Time goes by. He's still in the hospital. The gun is delivered. The guy calmly puts it together, lays it across the arms of his wheelchair, wheels himself to the window and kills the mill owner with one shot when he's walking home for lunch.

Served the bastard right, is what I say. There was a terrible outcry by the mill owners, big deal. They hung the guy, but so what? He didn't have much of a life left anyway. I feel a little sorry for the mill owner's wife and family, but not much. I'll tell you who I felt most sorry for—the logger's wife and kids. The mill owner's family had so much money by that time, they just moved up to Seattle to get out of the rain. Then their house burnt down, and they all died. Kind of makes you think about divine retribution, doesn't it? I know I should be more sympathetic, but what about the guy who lost his legs? They should have been looking out for him. If the Wobblies had still been around, they would have.

That's what Duke always said, and that's what I believe, too. If we don't look out for each other, if we don't take care—and make ways to take care—of each other, we are failing as human beings. I feel very strongly that our measure, as a country, depends on how we treat the least among us, not the best among us. Duke said that, too. And I agree with him. Duke never had much money, but what he had was guts and caring, and I'll take that over money any day of the week.

I would watch him at the baseball games after he would see these guys, when he would come back to be with me. And he'd shake his head and look out at the field, and one time I caught him crying, and I asked him why he was crying. He took me in his lap and cradled me, and I could smell his whiskey-cigarette-man smell, and I could feel the tears on his cheek and he said, I'll never forget it, he said "I was gone a long time during the war before you were born, and I saw a lot of people hurt and dying because I couldn't get them to the hospitals in time. I just don't think it's right that guys here, in peacetime, should not get taken care of."

And then he talked about the game and finally he put me back in my seat, but I remember it very clearly. Not just because I was getting older then, and he didn't pick me up and hold me as much as he used to before, and not just because it was one of the last times I was with him before he died, but really because he was right, and I could finally understand what he was doing and why it was so important.

He was a real man, my father was, a real man and a real father. A lot of people don't have real fathers, but I did. I had a real father once, and I don't care what people said about him after he died, he was a good father to me, and he was a good man. He worked for justice, which is a lot more than I can say for my stepfather.

My stepfather was, still is I guess, although I am not in contact with him anymore, my stepfather is a doctor—a surgeon. He works for several of the big mills, a company man. He met my mother when I was in the hospital for one of my many surgeries after the car accident. I was in and out a lot, and I get confused now which time it was, but anyway it doesn't matter. Fullman just picked my mother up one day as she was waiting in the hall; I figured it out when I was older. He just picked her up like a cheap date while she was supposed to be waiting for me. Later, she was surprised when he picked up other women. I suspect she's not surprised anymore. Well, she's made her own choices.

I don't think much about her anymore. But I think about Duke, and I think about him a lot. I remembered him so much this last time I was hurt. I dreamt about him a lot, and sometimes it seemed like he would come in the room and talk to me, and God, I missed him then. It's one thing to never have had a father, but it's another altogether to have had a father once and then to have lost him.

My father was a gorgeously handsome man, and I know if he were alive today, and I took him walking down Broadway, guys would fall over themselves. He was that kind of drop-dead black Irish poet type. And, I've wondered since I came out if he were gay, too. I don't ever remember him taking up with any of the women who were always hanging around him. He didn't pay them any attention, except in a sisterly sort of way. Maybe I'm idealizing him; I've thought about that too. But then again, maybe I'm not. All I know is, when I was with him, I was the center of the universe. And I knew that.

He really liked me. He liked how smart I was and always said I was the elf fairy princess. And when I felt bad because someone had teased me at school for reading too much, or said I was fat and couldn't play on their team, or when my mother would pull at my unruly hair so hard I would cry, he would take up for me. He would literally take me up into his arms and put his cheek next to mine and whisper in my ear that some day, other fairies would find me, and I would be treated like the true princess I was. That was an incredible gift for a man to give his daughter because I *was* different from the other kids, and I was very different from my mother.

I always *felt* like a princess with him; I was at home with him in a way I never was with my mother, and I don't exactly know how to explain that to you. Duke and I did things together. He taught me how to look at things and people. He taught me to fight for what was right, for other folks, and for those too small for everyone to see. He taught me how to do everything—except gamble. He taught me how to handicap, which I wasn't very good at because it involved numbers, but he never taught me how to place a bet. And he never gave me anything to drink, I mean, not alcohol, which is more than I can say for my stepfather, about whom I would rather not talk.

I loved my father. And I miss him. But what he gave me no one can take away from me. I, too, believe that everyone should have health care. And I'm working, and have been working all my adult life, to make that belief become a reality in this country. I know, when I come home from a long day at work, it doesn't really bother me because I can feel Duke's arms around me or passing me a plate of some really great food, and I can hear him saying, "That's my girl." And that's all I need, really.

I certainly haven't worked for money, although it would be nice to have some. That's what Duke would always say, and he never made any either. I think that's why he gambled so much, if you want to know the truth. My mother was always after him for more money, always after him for a nice dress for going to the club or something. She should have gone to work herself, made her own damn money. That would have been useful, at least. It would have given her something to do which, frankly, she needed. She just wasn't kept busy enough, especially after she married Roger. She just hung out at the club all day long and drank too much. She never drank too much with Duke, never, I can swear to that.

But I don't mind not having money, not really. I want things, just like everybody else, but I mean, what's the point? I need money now, to take care of my knee, and I certainly thought Harry Brice should have been made to pay about four times what his insurance company ended up paying, but that's not the same. I mean, I don't need a nice house or nice clothes. A nice meal every so often is good. This was a good idea to talk here, and I appreciate your picking up the check. I *will* have dessert, thank you. The sopapillas here are very, very good. God, I love good food, don't you?

No, probably not. You skinny girls never do. Show me a skinny woman, and I'll show you a woman who has trouble with her appetites. Duke never cared what I ate, which is more than I can say for my mother. Duke let me eat anything I wanted to eat, and he often took me places little kids never went—Chinese places; I had my first dim sum when I was about seven. I adored it, still do to this day.

That was the thing about Duke. He was never afraid to try anything, and I wish I was more like him that way. I, well God, I haven't talked about Duke this much in forever. I think about him, but I don't much talk about him. People don't really understand, do they? But you, you must have had a good relationship with your father, or you wouldn't have let me go on for so long.

The thing is, people don't really understand about universal health care either. This Clinton thing—what a bunch of crap. It's so piecemeal. It's *so* piecemeal as to be nothing. All the bones tossed to the insurance industry. Don't get me started on that.

It's bad enough I have to deal with the board—well, I mean when I was at the clinic. I'm remembering now the struggles we used to have to get the board involved with the mission of the clinic, and especially some of the meetings after it was discovered that Annie had taken so much money that we had nothing left to operate on. You think I was mad, ho boy, you ain't seen nothing until you've seen poor women or women of color find out that some middle-class white woman has taken their money and gotten away with it. There were women at those board meetings who just wanted to string her up, and frankly, I wouldn't have stopped them if I had thought it wouldn't hurt the clinic.

But see, that's what we had to keep in mind, what was going to be best for the clinic. That's why I resigned when I did. I felt very strongly that I couldn't do the kind of job the clinic needed done.

I remember trying to get ready for the board meeting when I was going to have to tell them about the embezzlement, and how bad it was. I can remember my leg was pulsating, it was so swollen and painful, and I can remember thinking that someone else should have been handling the problem, because really, I just couldn't concentrate. The amount of money that was taken made it a full-sized problem. I was only able to give it pint-sized energy. We needed to find an immediate source of funds to keep going even if I did go out on disability, so that my salary didn't have to be paid. We had to find an immediate source of funding, and we had to get a billing clerk in there right away. I had been trying to do the billing on the weekends, since Annie had been gone, and probably I should have hired someone sooner, but it just didn't work out.

So we needed to get someone right away, and I didn't need the board to tell me that. We needed to get money right away. And we did, in the end, from community fundraising, but I don't think we would have been able to make it at all if I hadn't gone on disability. So there were a couple of reasons I left. But it was never because I took money. God, it burns me when people say that. And to a reporter, no less. Annie Bartleby's one thing. The other women who pass this stuff along are just as bad; well, maybe not as bad, but just as useless.

When I think about the work we did at the clinic, the really valuable, healing work. Well, for example, I'll tell you about this one woman. She had advanced-stage breast cancer, spread to her vital organs, that kind of thing. And she didn't want to go to a doctor because she hated doctors. Well, okay. I understand that. Believe me, after all this, I really understand that.

So what did we do? Well, we connected her with the women in the group Jackie Winnow started before she died. God, I can't remember their names, but you know who I mean, so she'd have a support group to go to. And we got her hooked in with a lesbian oncologist over at the U. And we got her partner into a support group; we got them home health care.

And yes, she died, okay? But we were able to help in the

end, and that means something, you know? She wasn't alone when she died, and we helped her work her way through the system. Her partner wasn't just left there, hanging out to dry.

Maybe right now, that's as good as we can do. But the government needs to understand, if people don't come to healthcare, healthcare has got to learn to come to them and help them where they are. There is no standard way to deliver healthcare in this country, especially not for women. We worked really, really hard at the clinic to develop ways, innovative ways, to bring care to women.

And I don't care what anyone says, this is a dream worth having and working for. And frankly, I don't care who leaves that work for more money or whatever it is that they think they want in other places or with other women. Accessible healthcare is a dream worth working for and worth fighting for. People ought to be treated with dignity and care, and they ought to be able to use the healthcare resources that this country has made available to rich white men. And I don't care what I have to do to do it, I will have those things for women. In my way, I have been able to provide some of that for some women, but there is much more work that needs to be done, and even if I can never walk another step, I'll always be trying to find ways to further that dream.

Now, if we could talk about that, as a community, if we could get behind that the way we've gotten behind AIDS or making money to buy our little dream houses in the suburbs, if we could get together behind this very simple idea of making sure each one of us has simple access to good health care, then we could really do something together, something that mattered. The idea that women deserve to be taken care of is still, unfortunately, a revolutionary idea. Simple peace, simple justice. I've never understood why it has taken so long.

Laura

Was I this involved with all my clients? No. Not by a long shot. I was involved with my clients, yes. It was important to me to be involved. I had practiced law in a non-involved way all those years I was in corporate law. Corporate law defined the term "non-involved." Corporate law and the military may be the highest achievements of patriarchal society, if you want to call them achievements, and there are those who do. You can't get much more detached than corporate law. Even the money you make is detached from you—or at least it was to me. I remember looking at my paycheck one day and thinking to myself, well what am I going to do with this?

I think about that now, and I have to laugh. I could use a little of it now, that's for sure. We need to replace the main water line from the street! Sure, we need it now. But not enough for me to go back. What I have now, what I make now, what I do now is not embarrassing. I don't have to walk around wondering what I've done that might be construed as harmful. I'll tell you, in those days, the most fun I had with my money was giving it away, so in a way, I suppose what I do for a living now is not surprising.

But in those days, I used to read every single fundraising letter I got, and I read them word for word. I'd make a big pile in the middle of the table, some night when Rebecca was on call, I'd just stack them up in the middle of the dining room table and have at it. I'd put Satie's *Gymnopedie* on the record player and I'd bring Amanda's little crib out by the speakers, and the whole house would be peaceful. She'd sleep for a change, and I'd write checks until my hand got tired or until Rebecca came home, whichever was first.

Oh, she hated to see me do it. "Be more discriminating," she'd always say. "Put it in your retirement account, for God's sake. Or at least in Amanda's. If you have to give it away, put a lot into one thing where you can really make a difference," she'd finish up. "Make a donation where you'd get recognized" is what I always thought she really meant.

Well, I didn't want to. So I didn't. I didn't particularly want anyone to recognize me. I liked to think of the money like rain—not the seed and not the sun, but the rain that came down softly and encouraged things to grow.

Pretty romantic, right? Well, what can I say? I liked to do it, and I liked to do it my way. Like when we went to church, if I could ever persuade Rebecca to go to church, she would always like to go to coffee hour afterward. I hated coffee hour. I was a member, a regular member of the Pilgrim's Congregational Church for years, and never went to coffee hour by myself. It didn't seem like a thing I could do after I had just spent an hour praying. I don't go to church for the coffee.

You know, whenever I think about these things, which is not all that often now, but after ten years together and a child, you do tend to reflect every now and again, sometimes I think it was a miracle Rebecca and I lasted as long as we did.

I met her in college. Wellesley. Moved out here to get away from her. No, that's not true. Well, maybe it is. Rebecca was a complicated woman; I suppose she still is. I haven't seen her in years, but Nettie still keeps up with her some. I just couldn't. I tried, but I couldn't keep it up after what she did about Amanda.

Funny, isn't it—how one thing leads to another? You asked me if I were involved with all my clients as much as I was with Margaret, and the truth is no. But the truth is also yes, and there is a reason for that. Oh, this is beginning to sound like a conversation I would have with Nettie.

My best friend. Maybe the real reason I moved out here. I met her my first day at Wellesley, and I was just enchanted by her. She wore all black in those days, which stood out in its own way in the era of psychedelics. She was a mathematical genius, and she lived across the hall from me. She plays chess, or maybe more accurately, devours chess. The first year I knew her, we played chess fifty-two times, once a week, and I won twice, I think because she let me.

We still play. I've gotten better. She's gotten older. Sometimes, when she's tired, I win. She's been tired ever since she had the two boys, and even more so since she got rid of that louse she was married to. I feel sorry for straight women sometimes, don't you? Well, I suppose he was nice enough to look at, and I know that mattered to her, much to my sorrow. She would never believe how handsome she was.

Still is. Yes, we are still friends. I remember playing chess with her in the middle of Margaret's case. We only play about once a month now; she brings the kids down for the weekend, and they play with Joe, Brenna's boy, who lives with us part-time, but Nettie and I don't play chess on those nights. Those are family nights. We make sure to play, just us, about once a month, though, even if I have to go to Seattle. We always have managed to get together, except those ten years I lived in D.C. with Rebecca.

I remember a night during Margaret's case, playing chess with Nettie. Brenna and Joe had gone somewhere, maybe to the opera, which he loves. Opera and the NBA. I will never understand men. Or boys. Nettie says they are another species, and we are not meant to live together. She said this to me as she was gathering up the boys one night, and one of them, Geoff, says, "Mom, what is species?"

"Toothpaste darling, just toothpaste," she answered him which seemed, at the time, to work, although I know Mandy never would have fallen for that.

My goodness, I'm rambling tonight. You want to know what happened, what happened to me that affected my work with Margaret. I can tell you this story. We were still living in Seattle then, and Nettie came over on a winter night, not too long after I had accepted the case, but after I had gone to see Dr. Lennox, which I remember because I told her about it. We talked non-stop during dinner and then played mostly in silence after we had eaten, as was our custom. When she announced checkmate, she got up from the table, walked over to the bookshelf and pulled out a worn copy of the Dante we had read together in college, me tutoring her in English and her helping me in math.

She pulled out the volume and looked at me through her new half-glasses and began to read. I know it from memory now, so many nights I have read it since then.

"In the middle of the journey of life . . ." she began and then stared at me over the top of her glasses.

"Let me see that," I said, getting up.

She tossed me the book and said, "You never should have been in law, any more than I should have been married. *You* told me; now *I'm* telling you. Get out. I love you."

And then she wrapped herself up in her raincape, kissed me on the cheek, and let herself out. The house was very quiet, and I went to the window and watched the clouds moving over the lake. I stood there in the darkness for a very long time until I was so cold, I went to get a wrap. I turned on the light then and began to read, and the more I read, the more I began to believe that perhaps it was not too late for me, that I could make changes and survive. Nettie had. I could too. I had done it before, and I could do it again. There was life after corporate law, and there would be life after private practice. I just had to look for it.

The funny thing was, as Brenna pointed out later, I never used my law degree to fight for myself. If I had, I would have challenged Rebecca in court for shared custody of Amanda. But I couldn't. I wasn't sure I would win, not with what the courts were like in those days, even today. I was the non-biological parent. I had no rights, legally. When Rebecca said she was being generous to let me see her three hours a month, I knew a legal case could have been easily made for the truth of that.

But ten years is a long time to love a child. Long enough to know that at that age, shame about your parents begins to set in, and gets very strong in the next two to five years. Was I going to drag Amanda through that? What a Solomon's choice. I blinked.

I'm sure Rebecca knew I would. I always had before. She knew I would walk away from what I loved even if it hurt me, if I was doing it for someone I loved. She'd watched me do it with my tennis, because I loved her.

Yes. I was nationally ranked in college. I could have turned pro. This was before Shriver or Sabatini or any of the girl wonders, when women's tennis was still played by women.

It wasn't Rebecca's fault, and it wasn't her choice. If I sound like I'm blaming her, please know that I'm not. I made my own choices. I decided to go to law school because people in my family *did* something. People in my family did not play tennis, except on the weekend. But the women in my family gave up everything for the men they loved. And because much was given to me, much was expected of me; I was expected to give it back to the community. Law seemed like a good choice. I could, after all, read and write and think clearly. The truth is, I drifted into law because I thought that's what grown-ups did. They stopped playing tennis, they married, they had children, and they went to work. In my family, the women went to work *and* gave up everything for those they loved.

So that's what I did. It wasn't terribly creative, but then, that was never my strong suit. Rebecca went through med school, and I went through law school, and I got my first job just as she started her residency. I've wondered about that, too. Would I have gone into corporate law instead of advocacy law, as I had wanted to do, if we hadn't needed the money so much? Would I have gone into corporate law instead of advocacy law if there had been an opening at the local ACLU? Would I have gone if I hadn't been courted by men who looked like my father, who believed I did good work and told me so? Would I have gone if that firm hadn't had a branch in the city where Rebecca was going to do her residency? Wasn't I my mother's daughter?

I don't know. I know everyone was surprised. I know Nettie was furious, almost as furious as I was at her wedding. We both covered up pretty well, but not enough to fool the other. I told myself I would do pro bono work for whatever advocacy law firm needed me, at night, after my regular work. I don't know what was more foolish: saying that or believing it. I had no time after work. All I did was work.

All Rebecca did was work. When she wanted to have Amanda, I thought she was crazy. "When?" was all I could think. But she got pregnant, and my life suddenly changed from all work, to all work and childcare every other second. And maybe, for all I know, it was sleep deprivation that kept me in corporate law so long. That and bills. It's very easy to spend a lot of money when you have it. And Rebecca hadn't had very much when she was young, so Amanda got the best of everything: private schools and tutors, and I really can't believe she's turned out as well as she has, given all that.

God, it's interesting how much this all still hurts. I have missed her every day since the day I left her mother. When I finally left Rebecca, Mandy was about the age Margaret was when her father died. Don't think I didn't think about that. There were days when that was all I could think about. That and the limits of the law. How law is not about justice and not even really very much about power, but more about how much someone is willing to pay to be right—how much and in what currency. How the system works if you can work it and if you have the time, money, and determination to be the one who wins, never mind the cost to you or anyone else. How wrong how much of that is and how much destruction it has caused, how little it has to do with the human heart or healing or changing anything. It's only we who can change.

And the more I read Dante that winter, the more I understood what he meant about being lost in a dark wood. That time was sort of an inferno for me in the midst of cold, rainy Seattle as I contemplated the inevitability of finally and completely leaving the law. It would mean the compromises that I had made with myself along the way hadn't worked, and I was going to have to look harder, deeper for the truth about my life. I wasn't really sure I was up to it. I was forty, and I was afraid.

I had come to Seattle because Nettie said I could heal here in the rain. And because she was here and because I believed life was slower here and quieter and more possible. I thought I could go into private practice, a small practice, a limited practice, and do some good on a local level with real people. Do wills, co-habitation agreements, contracts, that sort of thing. I wanted some peace. I wanted to believe what I did mattered. I wanted to stop tormenting myself about Amanda and whether I had the right to leave her mother if it meant I left her, too.

I met Audrey almost immediately after I got to Seattle from contacts I had in the national gay and lesbian legal association. "Oh, look up Audrey Carr," they all said. "And tell her I said hello." That's how Audrey is known—by everyone and with positive feelings. She is one of the most gregarious women I have ever met. I just wish we were still friends. But maybe we never were, not really. It's understandable, I guess. She put a lot of effort into me. And I believe she genuinely liked me. Audrey is nothing if not genuine. As genuine as a person who has spent her whole life in law can be, I guess.

What does that mean? Sounded sort of ungrateful, didn't it? I didn't mean for it to. Audrey Carr really helped me put my life together in a way that I needed at the time. I guess what I meant was just that something happens to women who practice law. There is something damaging about the thinking, the way of compartmentalizing thought from feeling, intellect from soul, right from wrong. I don't know, maybe not for everybody. But certainly for me.

What I was desperately needing the winter I took Margaret

Donovan's case was a way to articulate those thoughts to myself so that I could see what had happened to me. Call it a mid-life crisis if you want to put it into journalistic short-hand. There were certain questions, I needed to ask myself. They were not altogether pretty questions nor were they easy. Was this life what I wanted? Was I the person I wanted to be? Was I happy? Did I feel whole? How had I gotten so lost?

Some of these were questions I had struggled with all my life. I am not like Audrey Carr or Margaret, for that matter. I have not always known what I wanted to do or why. I was not blessed with the kind of creative vision that Nettie or Brenna have. And I am not like my mother and father, although I have benefited from the wonderfully secure family background they gave me.

But I am not like my mother and father because I am a lesbian. And no matter what privilege my parents may have been able to buy me or convey to me or that I have been accorded due to my race or class, the things and people I love most in the world can be taken from me, legally taken with only a whisper of protest on my lips as an answer. Every lesbian knows this somewhere inside her, the way all women know they can, and may, be raped at any time.

I have known all my life I was a lesbian, but in many ways, I was protected—not from knowledge of danger, but from the actual danger itself. My mother knew and eased my heart when I didn't date, never asked me why I turned down the few offers I had, held my hand in my confusion, and never pressured me to marry. She protected me as best she could. I was protected when I came out at Wellesley. I was protected in my closet in corporate America, Washington, D.C. I watched as others took the heat in those early, heady days of the movement. But I was not protected in my own home. I learned things in my own home that I never wanted to believe were possible and never wanted my child to see were possible.

There were things my child witnessed that I never wanted

her to know: that people could be ripped from one another, even as they stretched out their hands to hold on; that her mother could not protect her from her other mother; that terrible things would be done in her name that had nothing to do with her at all; that people she loved would not tell her the truth. I could not protect her, and I have remained tormented about that. I have often wondered if I had known she would be shown these things, would I ever have left at all?

But I wondered those things, night after night, when all I *could* do was speculate. I spent my first year here in Seattle by myself, alone in a small house I had purchased with the money Rebecca had paid me for my part of the house in D.C. I sat alone, except for Nettie, and I wept, and I watched the rain. On Sundays, I went to church, and I ran out the second the service was over, glad to be back in the anonymity of the rain.

I studied for admission to the bar, and I met Audrey Carr, and a year after I had been here, I met Brenna at a craft show. We dated. I passed the bar. Audrey offered to share office space with me. I accepted. Brenna and I moved in together and I stopped crying all the time—just some of the time, and then as my work grew, less and less. And although we were living together, my work began to take me away, and we began to spend less and less time together. Even as I tried to heal myself, after a time I discovered, maybe like Nettie said, somewhere in the beginning, I had taken a wrong turn.

It took me many years to come to grips with that, and the end of it was when I was Margaret Donovan's attorney. It is not true that I gave her inadequate representation. There were many difficulties with Margaret's case. The timing in her case was just dreadful. But because I was so involved, I knew there were going to be complications of one sort or another, and often I knew them right away. I did the best I could to anticipate the problems and deal with them as they arose. But the problem was, I wasn't the kind of lawyer Margaret wanted.

I can tell you, from the work I've been doing as a regional

arts administrator here in Olympia for the last several years, I can tell you there are other attorneys like me. And I can tell you that there are many more like Audrey Carr, who do care to do what is right and who make an effort to do good work. But many women like me have been getting out of the law and some have done the critical work of setting up the ADR, a national body for alternative dispute resolution, for which I am very grateful.

More and more women seemed to be agreeing that the workings of adversarial law do not lead to the discovery of truth. They lead to the reward of one of two court-presented extremes. It wasn't hard to make extremes in Margaret's case— both Margaret and Harry Brice took extreme positions by themselves, if not right away, then certainly by the time they gave their depositions. Their depositions were among the most difficult and painful I had ever encountered. At least Margaret's was understandable. She was being attacked on all sides and, although I didn't know that before hand, I could see it from her reactions during her depo.

That she feels I turned and attacked her, too, is something I can not change, but that I sincerely regret. I remember realizing something was terribly wrong the moment I saw her come into my office for the depo. I wasn't sure exactly what had happened to her during the weeks between when I had seen Dr. Lennox and the time the depo was scheduled, but something had happened, and I knew it the moment I saw her.

I watched her come in, dragging her leg behind her like a maimed lion, and I remember thinking then she was much more wounded than I had known. If jackals were to smell the blood on her, they would be all over her in a second; all that was left was to rip her throat out.

Pulling the Loose Thread

Margaret

I was *not* asked to resign. That's a vicious lie. Honestly, I don't know where you get these things! Who have you been interviewing now? I was never, ever once asked to resign by the board at Hull House.

But I'll tell you one thing: if you are going to keep asking these kinds of questions, we might as well stop these interviews right now. Because, as I told you before, I think the press's emphasis on personalities over issues is disgusting and divisive, and I think it contributes to a lack of seriousness in our community. And a lack of focus on real issues.

And furthermore, I'm not going to spoil a good meal discussing such trivialities. I can tell you exactly what went on during the board meetings during that time, because, I would like to emphasize, I WAS THERE. Anyone else you may be talking to was, in all likelihood, not there, because if they were, they wouldn't be making up stories like this.

Of course, I will tell you what happened. Someone is still using you to get at me, though, and I don't really like it. You can say all you want that you haven't talked with Annie, but who else would be spreading rumors like this? If you heard it, there must be other people out there in the community who have heard it, and probably from her. Rumors spread like wildfire, and they are like snakes: you can't tell the end from the beginning. But I know where this one started. God, I hate that woman.

I tell you what I'm going to do. I'm going to sit here and study the menu for a moment and then when I'm done, we'll talk.

Okay. I'm sorry I got upset. I just . . . I hate it when people say things like that that simply aren't true. It just didn't happen. It's so far from what happened that I don't even know how to fight it. It's crazy-making. The distortions out there are so slimy and so removed from real life that I often wonder if these people have nothing to do but sit around and gossip about people who really are doing things. I mean, what do they do? Watch "Jeopardy" and Vanna White every night? I know one woman—this is a true story—I know one woman, a terrible gossip and a lesbian mind you, who keeps a notebook of every final "Jeopardy" answer and question set. Now, what kind of mind would do that? Only a very, very bored one, that's what.

It's the same kind of mind that sits and waits for those of us who are actually doing something to fuck up, and then they try to destroy us. And if we don't fuck up, they say we did, anyway. They just make up something, something totally not true, like this thing you just repeated to me. These women need to get lives of their own to fuck up. I wished they'd leave mine alone.

No! There isn't any part of it that's true. None of it. And I'll tell you one other thing! I'm glad I picked a sushi restaurant tonight because you are going to pay big for this interview. And write this down: the more you insult me with this kind of thing, the more expensive the dinners are going to get. Seriously.

Well, of course it's insulting. It's very insulting. This is an institution I built with my own hands, that yes, I was forced to leave, but not because the board forced me, but because a disability forced me.

I went to the board, let me see, I think it was about a week after the mediation hearing, and I told them I didn't know how much longer I could go on. But that wasn't the first they'd heard of it; I'd been warning them since I got hit. Of course, I did. I mean, I could hardly run the clinic from home. But they begged me to stay on.

Well, let me see. One time I remember clearly was right after the deposition, which, as it turned out, I was completely unprepared for. I mean, the second question they asked me was about my weight.

Talk about a total frontal assault. I was absolutely unprepared, which is one of the reasons Laura Gilbert is not my attorney anymore, I'll tell you that. She should have known they would attack me in a personal way. God knows, we spent enough time preparing in every other way. I certainly had no idea they would come after me like that. It was so blatantly aggressive. I mean, really—I didn't even understand what they were getting at.

Oh, they were just slime-molds. There were two of them, one man, one woman, both straight of course, and the woman looked like she was in another line of work altogether, sort of blowsy, do you know what I mean? There was a tear in the armpit of her jacket, and her skirt seam was crooked, and her hands were not clean. I mean, I was shocked to see that was all the representation money could buy. She hadn't even combed her hair before she came in. I don't really remember what he looked like except he had a shock of black hair over his forehead and glasses and little pig eyes.

They were late; I remember that. They kept me waiting and kept my attorney waiting with her clock ticking. Attorneys all seem to have clocks that keep on ticking no matter what they are doing, although I have never heard an attorney ask what time it was. I often wondered if Laura's clock ticked when she had sex. But anyway. We were waiting, and they finally came in.

So at first Emmie Slattery says nothing, only looks over Pig-eyes' shoulder, and then he clears his voice and starts his questions in a kind of monotone, and I'm thinking, okay, I can do this. I look over at Laura, and she smiles encouragingly, and then, thank you very much, he starts in on my weight. Well, I didn't answer.

In a deposition, you don't have to answer any questions you don't want to. And your attorney can object, which thankfully Laura did. She told me beforehand she wanted me to answer all the questions even if she objected to them, but *I* objected to the question. Furthermore, I don't have any idea what I weigh, then or now. I don't weigh myself, and I consider weight to be a tool of the patriarchy to oppress women. I don't think what I weigh is any more their business than whether or not I have sex. It's just not their business, and it is *not* a health issue, and I am sick, sick to death of hearing about it.

When my own doctor, now this is the doctor who did my surgeries, said during the mediation that my weight would affect the inevitable development of arthritis in my knee but would not cause the arthritis, I didn't know whether to kiss her or hit her.

I mean, the issue is just not relevant. I was hit by a car. The impact shattered my tibial plateau. I think we were not in disagreement on the basic facts of the case. But boy! What they did with that! I was so angry and flustered after the weight question that I had a hard time even following the rest of it.

I hoped I had been forceful enough about not answering

the weight question that maybe Pig-eyes would go back to his sty, but then Emmie Slattery took over.

Ruffling through her papers and looking at me over the most smudged half-glasses I'd seen in a long time, she asked me about the accident with Duke. She started off with, "I understand you were thrown from a car and previously injured on the same knee when your father was driving drunk."

Well, let me tell you, I was speechless. I really was. I mean, I knew my medical records were going to be part of the case, and Laura and I had gone over them extensively. To tell you the truth, I got sick of talking with her about what happened, but she said she wanted us to be prepared. Right.

I was not prepared for a question about my father from someone who looked like my mother after she'd come home from one of her Seattle shopping trips where she'd been drinking all afternoon at some downtown bar.

And that's another thing, just so you get the record straight. My father did not die in a drunk-driving accident. My father was not drunk that day. I repeat: I was there. I know what happened. My father was not drunk; he had a heart attack, and there was a coroner's report to prove it, which Laura certainly should have gotten when she was up in Olympia snooping around anyway.

But she didn't, and there I was with this Slattery woman asking me questions about my father. Now what, may I ask you, did that have to do with my knee? Well, it didn't. That was exactly the point. They just wanted to rattle me, and they did. Laura objected, but I was still very rattled and couldn't correctly answer some of the detail questions about when Brice hit me: the exact time of day, the weather, that sort of thing. I was so angry, I just couldn't.

And that detail stuff was the kind of thing I was prepared for. I mean, I remembered it, but they already had me. I was so distracted by their animosity. God, if I had known a person could be directly hostile and get paid for it, I might have had a new career for my mother! It was awful. And I was shocked. And I was angry that Laura hadn't prepared me better. She knew what was coming. She'd seen them before. This was only one of my complaints against her.

So I went home that night and my knee was aching because I couldn't put it up on anything during the deposition, and I remember lying awake in bed that night and thinking, boy—is the mediation going to be worse? I'd kill them all first. It had been a Friday afternoon depo, which Laura had deliberately scheduled because she thought it might get them done quicker.

But what I remember is that I went home that night to an empty house, and I just brooded. And wondered how I was going to get into work the next day to do the billing that had gotten so behind. Kore had moved in by then, of course, but she was working late that night and when Laura dropped me off at the house, it was cold and rainy and dark. Even though it was April, it was one of those days to remind you that spring had not yet quite arrived.

It was cold, and I was cold, and I dragged my sorry ass up the stairs, and the kitty-babies were crying because I had been gone for so long, and I don't even think I had supper that night. I think I took a pill and went straight to bed. At least it was warm there.

But I do remember that night, lying in bed awake in the middle of the night, with Kore sound asleep next to me breathing steadily, and thinking to myself, this is insane. I can't keep doing this, any of this. I'll never get well, and I just can't do it. I was facing another surgery in two weeks to take the plate out and close the wound, another round of heavy antibiotics, more physical therapy, a pool exercise program every day I didn't go to therapy, and I still wasn't off crutches. I just couldn't do it all. I was afraid if something didn't give, I'd never get well and that, after all this time, made me just crazy.

And so I stopped. I just stopped trying, and I hoped people

would understand that here I was, a health care professional, and I knew the value of taking care of myself, and I was going to do that. And if they didn't understand, well then fuck them. I mean, I deserved to get as well as I could. I deserved it.

There were several board meetings to work out the transition, and I stayed on as a volunteer, an unpaid employee for quite a number of months following. But after that depo, I knew I was going to have to fight for my life with those assholes, and I knew it was going to take a toll on me. And I just wasn't willing to give in to their intimidation. Laura Gilbert might have been, but I wasn't.

I remember the next day very well, maybe because the night before was so desolate. That Saturday, the sky had been washed clean, and it was open and blue and stretched all the way to China.

It was just gorgeous. And there I was up in the office, with fluorescent lights overhead, and in the morning paper there were articles in the sports section on the status of spring training, and I'm telling you, for the first time, honestly, I wanted out. My leg was pounding, and there was a monstrous stack of paperwork taking over my desk, and I just thought, no, I can not do this. I do not *want* to do this. As clear as I had been the night before, I was even more clear the next day. I decided I just had to say no to the board, give them some time to realize my answer was final, and let them make some plans. I called Barbara Chadwick, and we scheduled a board meeting for that very Monday night, which was a great response time from her, but the board let it stretch out for another two months.

It was at that board meeting I simply resigned. No more negotiation. I gave notice effective that night. And that's what happened. It was totally my decision. The board did not fire me, far from it. They begged me to stay and help with the transition.

There were no financial improprieties on my part. Annie

Bartleby stole money, but she stole something worse from me. That, combined with the pain in my leg, just crippled me.

Why, she stole my will to run the clinic. She stole my belief in myself and my willingness to work through anything to get to the end, for the clinic's sake. That's what Annie Bartleby did to me. She literally stole the clinic right out from under me, and she did it in a way no one would ever understand, the way a man will deliberately beat a woman in places where no one will be able to see the bruises.

Although I think Kore did. She saw. And I remember that Saturday afternoon when she came to pick me up, she folded her arms around my shoulders as I was sitting in my chair in tears, and I remember that she said to me, "Come on. Never mind. You shouldn't have to clean up after people anymore. Come on. We'll find you something better."

Because that's what I was doing, on top of everything else, was cleaning up after Annie Bartleby, because of the work she didn't finish. I mean, I know the clinic was mine, and it was my responsibility, but it's one thing to know that you have the ultimate responsibility, and another altogether to have to do everything yourself.

Well, really, none of that matters now. Really, it doesn't. Yes, all that happened, but look where I am now. I have a great job with the City, where I actually get benefits and a pension fund, just like real people. Think about this: I get sick days. I actually get to call in sick and get paid to get well, which is almost inconceivable to me.

The whole time I was at the clinic, I never took a day off, except after the accident. I mean, the whole seven years I was there, I never took a single day off. I worked seven days a week, fifty-two weeks a year. I had to. I couldn't take time off. If I wasn't there, then things just didn't get done. I mean, what were the NP's supposed to do? Put a sign in the waiting room that said, no receptionist today, please wait? We did have to do that once, but it wasn't like there was someone there to cover for me. I was it. I had to be there. And God, by the end, I was sick of that.

So now, this is funny, I hadn't really thought about this, but now I'm in a position equivalent to that queen I told you about, remember him? The guy who I had the appointment with the day I got run over? Well, I advise people on how to apply for grants, and I suggest agencies that might be able to supply services the city needs, and that sort of thing. It's a great job.

Well, it's a bureaucratic job, but who cares? I take lunches now, which is a miracle, really. The whole time I worked at the clinic, I never got lunch. I mean routinely, I did not get lunch. Honestly. I got there at eight, and I worked until ten, unless I had a meeting. I worked every weekend. I never got a vacation. And here, I get two weeks paid a year.

Which is not to say I don't miss the clinic. I do. I miss it every day. And I would go back in a second, if I were young enough. But that kind of organizing is a young woman's job. I just can't do it anymore. I couldn't keep up with the physical demands; I couldn't walk enough to keep that job now.

But I miss it. Sure I miss it. I wasn't asked to resign. I left on my own two feet, limping as I do now. But I blame Annie Bartleby and Harry Brice for taking it away from me. It's all water under the bridge, but I don't forget, and I don't forgive. I remember exactly what happened.

Laura

I'm not exactly sure when I began to be afraid for Margaret. Perhaps it was there even before I went to see Dr. Lennox. I know there was a certain feeling of inexplicable necessity propelling that visit. I did not stop to think about it at the time; suppression of feeling is a cultivated asset within the legal profession. And to admit one is afraid for a client implies a certain lack of confidence in one's own abilities to control the situation. To have been able to face that during the time I was representing Margaret would have been impossible. The arrow of time flies in one direction only.

And to have said I was afraid for Margaret would have made an implication Margaret would not have liked at all. Nonetheless, I do remember exactly when I became aware of the existence of that feeling. It was during the weekend in between depositions, after the depo I conducted of Brice, but before Margaret's depo was scheduled.

Well, a deposition is basically part of the building of a formal legal record. What that means is that an attorney will go to an individual with the intention of getting information in the form of a sworn statement. There is a court reporter present and opposing counsel. The attorney who is the deposer, that is, the one who called for the deposition, usually asks most of the questions; opposing counsel has the right to ask follow-up questions to clarify any point that might be germane to her client's position, and then the deposer gets one more chance to follow those questions. The person being deposed is sworn in by the court reporter and a transcription of the deposition is treated as though it were testimony given in court.

Most of the time, attorneys are not hostile to the person being deposed. I certainly have always felt that it serves no useful purpose to antagonize any witness. On the other hand, attorneys as a group are no more alike than any other class of people.

In other words, yes, some of us are arrogant, hostile, and intent on forced domination as a lifestyle choice, and some are not. I personally would not call them assholes, but I understand the classification of your terminology.

Certainly, Harry Brice's lawyers fit into that mold. The attorney from his insurance company had been, all along, unusually uncooperative. As I said earlier, he had rebuffed my initial overture for immediate settlement, claiming his client's automobile had been damaged by my client's negligence. I had initially figured this to be part of a standard strategy of intimidation, which didn't bother me excessively. I was, in fact, somewhat amused by his spin on events. Although I had seen its cousin often enough in corporate and government circles and was not unfamiliar with it, it was unlikely enough to be used in a case of so little public consequence that it still made me smile.

But when I had called to cancel the Lennox depo, my effort to save him and his company time and money had been met with rude insinuations of incompetence, and I just decided I wouldn't even try to be friendly, while remaining open to the possibility of rapprochement.

I suppose I needn't have bothered, but I would rather err on the side of being open than being closed. It takes a while for me to decide if rudeness is a temporary or permanent condition, and even if permanent, a person can change. At least I like to think they can.

I thought it safe to speculate that the attorney for Harry Brice's insurance company may not have felt at the top of his chosen profession and perhaps was part of the not small group of people who feel they can disguise in rudeness what they lack in mental abilities. It's so hard to know someone's motivation for certain, and not very useful, either.

In any event, I had most of my doubts on that score removed by the end of Brice's deposition. There were actually two attorneys at Brice's depo, about which I was quite surprised: one male representing the insurance company and one female representing Dr. Brice's personal interests. I would not say that it was absolutely necessary to have two attorneys do the job of one, but there are certain individuals who would rather spend more money to make sure they are not about to have money taken from them than they are concerned about exactly how much money is going out the door. In other words, robbery is of more concern to some people than actual loss, which seems short-sighted at first glance, but again, motivation is, by nature, often circumspect.

However, I was certainly not going to suggest to Dr. Brice that he was perhaps paying too much for representation, especially when he claimed to be unavailable for deposition except at 6:30 a.m. on Thursday mornings.

After Amanda was born and Rebecca was on call, there were many months for me of being up all night with only fragments of sleep in the manner of any mother. It was my first real understanding of the trauma that must have been done to Rebecca's psyche during her residency. I had never been an early riser. From Mandy's first two years until she learned to sleep through the night on her own, or at least comfort herself back into sleep, I have moments of terror of being awake at 6:30 a.m. I'm worried that it means I've been up all night, that there is someone I love who lies inconsolable nearby, and I become immediately exhausted.

For those reasons, I generally find it unwise to try to work at that hour, but Dr. Brice—a very busy physician indeed— insisted he had no other time and as an opening hostile gesture, I would say it was fairly effective. Nonetheless, I was prepared and awake and determined not to be insulted in any manner.

He had also insisted that the depo be taken in his office, as to further cut down on the time he was "being compelled to waste." I had no objection; as you may have guessed by now, I was interested enough in people to want to see what his office might look like.

I was left waiting in the hallway of the deserted medical office building for fifteen minutes past the scheduled start time and was not even invited in to the office waiting room where I might have gotten some of my own work done; but again, I was determined not to be thrown off by animalistic domination rituals. If one does not dance, one can't have one's toes stepped on.

Finally, the court reporter and I were admitted into the sanctum sanctorium, where Brice and his attorneys had been having coffee. There were two oversized chairs arranged in conversational placement, thick hunter green carpet, and a huge mahogany desk Brice sat behind, his face haloed in framed certificates and diplomas. Very effective, I thought. The leather-bound medical journals. Soft light from indirect halogens bounced off the ceiling. So, this was the office of a plastics man. Very different from my dad's office, which was austere by comparison.

Still, there was something similar. Something. Maybe Brice's tone of voice. I had heard it before.

He was brisk, abrupt, and as confident as only a surgeon can be. He had been doing less than the speed limit. He had been braking for the crosswalk. He was aware she was locking her car as he came close. When she turned and walked directly into his path, he hadn't even had time to sound his horn.

The visibility had been fine. He had not been tired. He had not had a large lunch. He had consumed neither coffee nor alcohol at lunch. He had not taken his eyes off the road. He had not had an accident since he had been a teenager. He was on no medication. His judgment had not been impaired in any way.

He could think of no reason why my client had run into his car except that she was obviously used to throwing her weight around.

Opposing counsel seemed to find this amusing.

She had done a great deal of damage to his new car. Had his attorneys spoken to me about a counter-suit?

Completely ignoring him, I turned to the opposing counsel and said I had no more questions, if they would like to clarify any statements, they should go ahead.

Well, yes, they certainly would. "What exactly happened?" they asked. I was amused to watch him drum his manicured and buffed fingers on the ridge of his mahogany desk.

"She walked into my car," he said in a dry tone.

"Had you been injured in any way?" the woman asked. I turned to give her a longer look than I had previously and was surprised to see someone who took no more care than she obviously did with her personal appearance to be representing someone like Harry Brice.

Brice seemed irritated too. "You have my medical records for a neck injury," he scolded her.

I raised my eyebrows at the insurance company attorney. "You were planning to make those available at some point," I said pointedly.

He brushed me off. "Doctor, would you say that if your car hadn't been forcibly stopped by a two-hundred-and-fifty-pound woman walking into your path, you and I wouldn't be here this morning?"

I watched his face as he said this. He was enjoying himself. I turned to Brice. He was bored and impatient. I looked at the woman. She was smiling too.

"I hardly think so," Brice said, clipping his words. "Are we done with this?" he asked, more as a statement of dismissal than as a question, and turned to his desk.

I had nothing further to say except to thank him for his time and give the office one last look as I packed my notes into my briefcase. Perhaps it was the smell that reminded me of my father. Brice had begun making chart notes, so closure had clearly already been accomplished for him. I went to extend my hand to the opposing counsel, who had their backs to me, and did not turn when I approached them.

I turned away and walked out, my head high, went home and took a shower before going in to the office.

It was certainly not the first time I had encountered such behavior from attorneys or people in general. There seems to be a direct ratio between the amount of power an insecure person has managed to accumulate and the amount of rudeness and rigidity they often need to express. I didn't take it personally.

But I realized, somewhere in the middle of a Saturday craft exhibition through which I was strolling on my way to Brenna's booth, that Margaret was very likely to take it personally. And I made a mental note, as I looked at some cobalt-glazed porcelain, that even if I were to prep her perfectly, what she might do in the moment of fire with them, with their animal level stupidity married to their smirks, was probably beyond my control. My heart sank into my stomach. I could watch the case deconstruct before my very eyes. But maybe not. I still felt as though I didn't have any kind of accurate reading on Margaret at all. Her moods and medications had been so unpredictable.

We were, by then, almost five months post-accident. Margaret was facing surgery the following week to remove the L-shaped plate Dr. Lucy had bolted into her tibia to hold it together. They had finally been able to control her infection, and after the plate came out, they would be able to get rid of it altogether. Margaret was three-fifths of the way home, but I knew she didn't feel like it. When I tried to make an appointment with her to prepare her for her deposition, she had claimed only to have an hour, as she was so backed up on her work that she just wasn't able to get anything done.

She came to my office almost two hours late, just as I was starting to lock up, and she startled me with the whiteness in her face. I let her in, and she dropped into the armchair in my office with a deep sigh, closed her eyes, and didn't speak for several long minutes. She reached down to her knee brace and began ripping the velcro open, saying, "I'm so sorry I'm late Laura, things just got away from me. You still have time for me, don't you?"

She stopped then, mid-way through taking her brace off. I knew she had me.

"It's hurting you, isn't it?" I asked, pulling the coffee table toward her so she could put her leg up. "You can't keep standing me up like this," I said, trying to soften my words.

"Oh, I know it. I'm so sorry," she said. "Could you get me a glass of water?"

I smiled to myself as I went out of the room. What a piece of work Margaret Donovan was, I thought, while mentally trying to calculate how much longer this would take and did Brenna say she would be home for dinner or not? It was Thursday afternoon. You might remember, I had been up at the crack of dawn that day, and I was tired, but if not then, when?

I got water and returned. She lay with her head against the back of the armchair, her eyes closed again.

"Here you go," I said. She took the glass from me, drained it, and handed it back to me. "More?" I asked.

She shook her head. "Listen, I appreciate you staying. Let's just get this thing over with, okay? I know you'd like to get home, and I would too."

She seemed so worn out that night, I had the impression her skin was as soft as a ninety-year-old, but it may have been only the late light. I started anyway. I was tired, too.

I began with a brief description of what a deposition was, similar to what I told you earlier. She nodded impatiently.

"Well, what about today?" she asked. "Tell me how it went with Brice."

Although I had prepared myself for this question from her, or at least its answer, I wasn't sure I wanted to start our hour together discussing it, but there seemed no way around it. It was then that I realized I was having a bad feeling in my stomach, but I pushed it away. She deserved to know what they were up to.

"They seem to think you are entirely at fault," I said, "If you can believe they think that's a defense."

She looked at me with her mouth open. "They can't get away with that, can they?" she asked. "I mean, how dare they!"

I laughed. "Don't worry," I said. "It doesn't mean a thing.

They just want to get your goat; they want to insult you into making a mistake. Don't fall for it, okay?"

She gave me her thousand-watt smile. "Why Miss Scarlet, I don't know nothing about birthin' no babies," she said.

I shook my head.

"*Gone With The Wind?*" she asked.

"Not me," I said.

"Oh God, my favorite book and second favorite movie. Duke had given me the book just before the last ball game we went to, and I read it over and over in the hospital."

"Well, do what you have to do to not rise to their bait. I'm serious, Margaret," I said as I went through my papers looking for my depo prep form. I looked up, and she was looking at her nails and then raised her eyes to me.

"Yes Ma'am," she said. Again, I felt like she was flirting, and I pulled away emotionally, going through the form as though I had complete confidence that she could handle what they gave her, as though she could be as dispassionate as Brice. We finished up in thirty minutes, and I dropped her off on my way home.

It wasn't until Saturday at the craft fair that I was able to process that meeting; I'd been in court all day Friday. Walking through the fair, wasting time until Brenna could get away to take a break, I reasoned that there wasn't anything I could have done to begin with. Margaret was Margaret. She was going to do what she was going to do. I had done my best to prepare her, or at least I felt I had done the best I could, given who Margaret was. Perhaps that was rationalization. Because my instincts were right on target. The depo was a disaster. But it wasn't nearly as bad as the mediation.

June
Swoon

Margaret

I just want to say: being hit by Harry Brice wasn't a total loss. I mean, I never would have met Kore if he hadn't hit me, and I hadn't needed so much care. There is a part of me that misses those early days with Kore; sure, don't we all miss the early days of any relationship? There was something we had then that we have never been able to recapture, and I miss it. I mean, it was a terrible time for me, what with the lawsuit and the clinic and all that, but there was such magic between Kore and me! Not that there isn't now; I don't mean that. But it was different somehow, and when I think about the mediation, I think too about those days in the garden the month before.

Seattle in the winter is no place to be, although it's better than where I grew up. Still, by February, murders are committed because people can't stand to see the gray anymore. But July and August are the ransom we get for those other lost months, and sometimes there are parts of May and June that act just like July and August. I don't complain if things get out of order, or if we get more summer than what's called for on the schedule. And believe me, after growing up where I did, well, I just soak it up. I can't get enough of it.

Why, the sun comes out and dries up all the rain. Not completely, of course, but oh! Seattle in the summer. Even when the sky is overcast in the spring, you can see how it's going to be—the colors of the flowers and the flowering bushes are accentuated like color television after only watching black and white for your whole life. The brightest reds, pinkest pinks, coral so vibrant it could cut you. You haven't seen spring until you've been in Seattle. By the time June comes, the light stays in the sky from five a.m. until 10 p.m. and there are longer and longer stretches when the weather is warm and lovely.

That year, we got a couple of tastes of summer early, particularly in May, after the surgery to take my plate out, and on into June. Kore would help me out to the garden, and we would lie there behind the evergreen hedge where no one could see us, not even the wind could find us. We would lie there, in shorts and sweatshirts to begin with (of course we pulled our shirts off after awhile), and my poor, sickly pale knee with its angry pink scars and puny little muscles would find some peace. I never slept the whole night through during the first year after the accident. Even if Kore was with me, the nights I did sleep were filled with nightmares.

More than anything else, that's what I remember about that first year—the pain and the exhaustion. I would wake up more tired than when I went to sleep. When it got really bad for me, and the sun was out, Kore would bring me out to the garden, and we would lie there together for hours without talking, just holding hands. And by and by, Kore would rub my knee if it was aching, which was often. And she would stretch me, and the sun would cook me, and we would lie there holding hands, and pretty soon I would start dozing off. It was the only time I got any sleep all that year. I felt absolutely safe there with her in the sun, and it was the sweetest time I have ever known in my life.

Kore had moved in with me about a month after she had first come to take care of me. She was staying overnight most of the time by then anyway, and her old housing collective was falling apart, and it just seemed time. I was so in love with her then. I have never felt so taken care of. Plus, I needed help with the rent, and she needed a cheap place to stay, and we had been lovers for a couple of weeks by then anyway, and it just worked out very well for both of us.

Well, I'm trying to remember when, exactly, we became lovers. It's so hard to fix a time or date with those things, don't you think? I mean, was it when we first kissed or when we first wanted to kiss or when we first slept together? Boy, now you talk about having to plan something in advance. With my leg and her schedule and the I.V. schedule, we did have to be aware of what was going on. It wasn't just, oh, fall into bed like it is for some folks. We knew exactly what we were doing. And the sex wasn't all that great anyway, on account of my leg, but you know what? It didn't really matter.

A lot of women talk about sex in the first year of their relationships as though it was the be-all and end-all. To tell you the truth, sometimes I think we just make that stuff up because we live in this male culture where sex is supposed to be God. Well, I think there are a lot of us who aren't that male identified and don't see our relationships as conquests but as mutual delight and softness and reassurance. And of course, you can get that with sex—don't get me wrong, I like sex—but on the other hand, sometimes there is just that sweetness, that feeling of being safe that is better, far better than any orgasm I've ever had. To tell you the truth, sometimes holding hands has been the best sex—and if you don't think holding hands is sexy, you are more deprived than you can imagine. It's beyond sex. It's the ultimate intimacy, and I had it with Kore during that May and June.

It's not that we don't have it now, because we do, sometimes. But you know, I'm working now, and my leg is what it is; it isn't going to change. In those days, I still believed that I would get better, that the knee would come back the way it had the first time, and that between me and Kore and the doctor, we could heal it. By June, the incisions had healed completely, and the infection was gone, but I had a sort of useless stick that I dragged around behind me, like a branch that wouldn't bear flowers. Still, I wasn't afraid then. I was tired, but I was determined. I went to physical therapy three times a week; four times a week I forced myself to go to the pool to do my exercises. And Kore was so great in those days. She would come with me and help me and make me feel not embarrassed about how I looked in a bathing suit. I mean, this woman took care of me in every way.

And too, during those days, I believed it was only a matter of time for the lawsuit to come to conclusion. I had agreed on mediation to begin with, after Laura said it would be quicker. Her fees would be reduced, and since it was an open-and-shut case, she thought Brice's attorneys were probably just blowing smoke and being ugly to save face while hoping to settle. She thought they might jump at the chance to settle. Well, I wanted to believe her. I needed the money, and I really wanted to get it over with. After the depo, I just wanted the whole thing over with.

There was a lot I wanted to believe in those days. More than anything else, that's what you should write about me: that I was gullible. I mean, I hired Laura because I heard she was the best. I trusted my former lover not to steal from me. I believed that if I was struck by a car driven by a wealthy man with insurance that I would get some kind of compensation. Maybe I was a fool.

Oh, it hardly matters now, not really. None of it matters

now. I'm certainly not the first person in the world to have been screwed by the American legal system. And probably not the first to be outraged.

Well, it *was* an outrage. I remember the day of the mediation very well because it was hot. It wasn't just "warm for Seattle." It was hot like summer, about 85 degrees, and people were panting on the buses. I was still walking with my cane then because I was off balance so much, and I wasn't driving because I couldn't keep concentrated weight on my knee. I remember getting out of the mediation and walking away from Laura because I couldn't believe what she had just told me, and I remember going down from the mediation lawyer's offices, over on Second Avenue, walking over to the underground stop in Pioneer Square and going down into the underground, where it should have been cool, but wasn't, and I remember wanting to run, to just run away from all of them and lose myself in the Friday-afternoon-going-home crowd and that's what I did.

I wedged myself into a car going out to Queen Anne and Ballard; I didn't really care where it was going, and I pushed my way on the car with my cane and my bulk. I'll tell you, sometimes being big can be a good thing, and I felt like pushing my size around that afternoon. I felt like crushing all of them.

And I got on the car and the crowd pushed back as soon as the doors closed, and I didn't even care. The sweat smells of hot, tired folks folded around me, and I just rode out to Queen Anne. I rode to the end of the line, and then I rode back downtown and changed for my bus to Capital Hill, and I went home.

Kore met me at the stairs and helped me up and didn't press me when I said I didn't want to talk and didn't press me during dinner, which was, as I recall, a beautiful pasta salad mounded up on a bed of spinach, with fresh bread, and nice flowers on the table, and I'm telling you I enjoyed it. Kore had gotten it for me, and I intended to enjoy it and I did.

I enjoyed my dinner and the ice cream we had afterward,

and I took a cool bath, and Kore put the fan on, and I lay down to rest almost immediately after. And she did not press me once, not once. I think I was finally able to talk about it sometime the next day, and I think it was out in the garden. I was so angry and so disappointed that I just about couldn't get the words out.

Well, basically they humiliated me is what they did. That's what the entire mediation was about. They didn't have a case, so they decided to humiliate me. Oh, they talked about my father and the previous accident, which—in my opinion—they never would have known about if Laura Gilbert hadn't been totally out of bounds in her research on the case. I mean honestly. They never would have found the previous medical records if she hadn't so conveniently gone and found Dr. Lennox, and even though he said there should have been no residuals, they sure made the most out of the whole story. And even though Laura kept objecting, saying something about the thin-skull ruling, no one paid any attention to her, as nearly as I could tell.

So there was that—"the previous injury," as they called it. And then they started in on the weight issue, which was not an issue until they made it one. And Laura kept objecting to that too, but the mediator didn't seem able to listen to her.

"Do you have an expert witness willing to testify that her weight won't have any affect on future medical?" he asked her at one point, as though I were not even in the room.

And then, when they claimed I walked out in front of Brice's car, I just about lost it. They claimed they had an accident engineering specialist to go out and measure probable impact point to skid marks and said I couldn't have been in the crosswalk.

Well, that just about tore it for me. Here again, we have people who were *not there* trying to tell me, *who was there*, what happened. I went ballistic. I didn't say anything because Laura had made me promise not to say a word unless I was spoken to—that's how childish that whole system is, how childish and how thoroughly patriarchal. I haven't been told that I wasn't to speak unless spoken to since I first lived in Roger Fullman's house. It was ridiculous and insulting. But I kept my tongue. And I kept waiting for Laura to do something. Do anything. But she just sat there, too. It was outrageous.

And that was their whole case. It took them three fucking hours of presentation to get to those three twisted points. And guess who they went after to make those points?

"When was the last time you weighed yourself, Ms. Donovan?"

"Can you tell us just how long you were in the hospital when you sustained your initial permanent injury to this site?"

"How many steps are you saying you took to get into the crosswalk, Ms. Donovan? Oh, you can't remember? Then perhaps you didn't. Perhaps all of this is just part of the case your attorney has orchestrated to get you more money, isn't that possible, Ms. Donovan?"

I want to tell you, I couldn't have possibly answered them then, even if Laura hadn't told me to keep my silence. Right now, I can't think what else to tell you about it. You can't fight back; Laura had spent hours coaching me after the deposition debacle. You can't tell them they are asking stupid questions. You can't tell them they are acne on the butt of God for doing this kind of work, that they are store-bought men, both the male and female, and that they deserve whatever hell they get when they come home to their empty houses and cheap dates who want expensive wine. Fuck them all.

I'll tell you what I did. I went home. And Kore took care of me. Because there wasn't anything else to do, really. There wasn't anything else to do. I couldn't believe that Laura had even let them make an offer after the mediator had said it would take him a week to issue an opinion, which wasn't binding anyway. I can't believe, even now, that Laura thought we could get anything out of mediation. I still wonder if she hustled me out of a jury trial because she had lost her nerve and knew she herself couldn't go with it and win, or whether she was just a bad lawyer.

She hustled me, I'll tell you that. She hustled me as much as the other attorneys did. She didn't want to be a lawyer anymore, did she tell you that? She didn't want to, but she kept on anyway. I guess she was looking for the one big score to put her out to pasture, but at the rate she was going, with the kind of chip shots she was getting from cases like mine which should have been big cases, I mean *really* big, well, she wouldn't have been able to retire until she was dead.

She just didn't do her work is what I mean. I mean she did too much work on finding the records and not enough work on getting people to testify for me. Experts on knees, experts on the effects of weight (like any exist!), witnesses who saw me walking in the crosswalk, that sort of thing. She must not have put up notices for witnesses on Broadway, like she said she did, for one thing. You know Broadway and the streets around it were just packed at five on a weekday afternoon. I remember people surrounding me when I came to after being hit. I mean, putting up notices to find witnesses is just a logical thing to do, and it doesn't take a rocket scientist to figure it out. If she had put them up, someone would have come forward. That was the thing with Laura; I felt like I was having to run my own case. I hated it then, and it makes me mad still to think about it.

And I've had a long time to think about what she should have done or could have done, and I have thought about it. A lot. But in the end, it doesn't matter, does it? I mean, where were we? I had just gone through one of the most excruciating verbal exchanges of my life where I was not allowed to defend myself. I could not speak in my own behalf. All I could do was answer yes or no. If I tried to answer more, I only made things worse. I could tell from the look on the mediator's face that he wanted me to shut up every time I answered back. I felt like I was watching my mother at the dinner table with Roger, and I was saying all the wrong things, and she wished, not for the first time, that I was as dead as Duke.

Believe me, I know that look. So I watched him all afternoon and watched my own counsel, ineffective at every turn, and watched myself and my knee twist in the wind. It was humiliating, and I hated them all for it, if you want to know the truth; I hated them all. Not one of them had gone through the hell I had gone through just to be able to walk into that room. For them to sit there and say I had made it all up or done it deliberately just drove me insane.

And then, when I caught sight of Laura in the hall with them, all I could think was, once a lawyer, always a lawyer, and if I'd had the guts, I would have spit on her right then.

But I didn't, did I? No, I couldn't. I mean, I could have, but what good would it have done? I remember the dream I had when I lay down in the heat that night; I remember it like it was yesterday. It was the beginning of a series of dreams, and if Kore hadn't been there, I would have screamed myself silly and woke up the entire street. As it was, I scared the hell out of her when I sat up, straight up she said, and began screaming, "Get out, get out!" at the top of my lungs.

I dreamed it was summer in Olympia, and I was in my shorty nightgown that my mother had bought me for my sixteenth birthday. God, I hated that nightgown. I was thin that year, had just finished my first big diet, and my mother had bought me that nightgown to celebrate, so I would never get fat again, she said (the bitch). And in my dream, I was lying on top of the sheets in my pink bedroom (which I detested) in Roger Fullman's house.

And in the dream, somehow, Roger had his dick in his hand and was rubbing himself and was saying "It's all right, baby, you know you want it. Just give me a little and then you can stay. You'll do that for your mom, won't you?"

And in the dream I remember feeling scared in my nightgown, on top of the sheets because it was hot, and with nothing to cover myself and looking at Roger and knowing I was going to have to do what he was asking because we had no money and hadn't had any since Duke died. I knew that, I knew how worried my mom was, because she told me all the time how terrible Duke was to have left us this way, and how she didn't know where we would go without a roof over our heads, and that she could just die from the humiliation of it all, and how she didn't, honestly didn't, know what she was going to do.

And in the dream, I saw my mom's pinched face and Roger's obscene penis. And then I looked down at myself, looking for something to cover me, and I saw my leg, all shriveled like a dead tree limb, and I knew I couldn't even run away from him, and I looked at him again and I guess I began screaming.

Even now telling you, I can feel it. I can see him standing there at the end of my bed, silently waiting for me to wake up. It took hours for Kore to calm me down. And you know what, it went on, night after night after night. Sometimes I was younger, much younger—ten, eight, seven—and there was Roger, always Roger. Him at the end of the bed and me trying to drive him off. I got so tired, I would see him in the daytime, on the streets, I could feel him, could feel his hands on me, especially on my knee, could hear him saying, "No man is ever going to want a woman with a leg like this. You're lucky I would even look at you, much less touch you."

And I began to believe it really happened. I began to think that something had really happened between me and Roger and that the stress of the new injury had brought up all these old memories to the surface, and to tell you the truth, I began to get crazy.

Although, I must say, the settlement amount Brice's attorneys offered was enough to make anyone crazy. They offered me a settlement of about one-third what I had been suing them for. Laura was advising me to take the money and get out of the process; she didn't think we'd get better, even if we went into binding arbitration, and in fact, we might do worse, plus I would have to go through everything again, and her fee would go up.

I was having these nightmares that were so real, I couldn't tell what was real and what wasn't real. And the clinic was falling apart. It was absolutely falling apart. Kore wanted me to go into therapy with this incest specialist she'd heard about, and Laura wanted me to settle, and there was a buzzing in my head and a pulsing in my knee that never went away.

And so, if I sat out in the garden in the sun and tried to find my way back to life, and if those moments out of the wind with Kore were the best times of our relationship then or since, well, maybe you will understand if I just say that I was tired. I was so tired. And I could rest there, just holding hands with a woman who loved me. I hope no one will begrudge me that. Try to understand, it was the only peace I got that whole year, and I deserved it. God knows, I deserved at least that. I didn't even know who I was, they had beaten me down so far.

Laura

There were roughly two months between the depos and the mediation hearing, and I didn't see Margaret very much during that time. She had her plate surgery; her doctor said she was doing very well. There had been a little shifting of the reconstruction due to the infection, but they had been able to control the infection before too much damage was done, and basically, she expected Margaret to make a good recovery if she continued with her physical therapy and rehab. She would be glad to put this all in a legal report if I would forward prepayment and thanked me very much for prepayment on the phone call.

I laughed and said, of course, that I would send it directly and thought to myself that a retainer seemed a bit easier as a way of doing business, but I didn't say anything. I did want the report, and I wanted it soon because, wonder of wonders, Margaret had agreed to a mediation. I was, frankly, a little surprised when she agreed. I had expected that her anger after the depo would keep her pragmatic business sense in the background, but I was wrong. Certainly wasn't the first time I was wrong about Margaret, nor was it to be the last.

I went ahead and negotiated with the equally surprised attorney for Brice's insurance company and got in line for a mediator, hoping for someone who was actually interested in mediation as a way of settling disputes as opposed to someone who was looking to build up chits in the community. That had hardly ever happened. The mediators were usually paid about half their hourly wage for mediation work, but I had had the experience of getting a few guys who had different agendas than the rest of us at the mediation, and it would just be Margaret's luck to draw someone who was having a bad day.

Well, I'm not sure it was anything I did that convinced her to do the mediation. I had been plugging mediation all along. It cuts attorney fees in half, and it was a very unusual case where the plaintiff was not awarded some reasonable fee—usually less than they might have wanted, but often more than they would have gotten had the case gone to trial, if only for the savings on the attorney fees alone. And then, of course, with a jury trial, there is always the chance that a person might lose altogether.

But even with a favorable judgment, the plaintiff is going to pay. It costs quite a bit of money to bring a case to trial. It has been my feeling for a long time that the people who eventually end up winning in court are those who have the money and emotional resources to keep standing, to keep slugging it out. Those who don't have the money to pursue the case, or to even hire adequate representation to pursue it for them, don't get justice in this country unless they have a happy meeting with fate or chance. Those cases, by definition, end up being news in the afternoon paper. They certainly don't happen every day.

But we have this idea that Ed McMahon is going to knock on our door someday, too. Hey, it has to happen to someone. I haven't decided whether this is optimism that springs so eternally in the human breast or just another instance of the human fragility of greed exploited and painted up nice by the magic of capitalism. God knows, I order the magazines, too.

But apparently some of my lectures on ways and means must have made some sense to Margaret, or perhaps she was not, unlike her father, the gambling kind. I didn't know and I didn't care. The idea of Margaret being cross-examined on the witness stand by Brice's attorneys in front of a jury was not a pleasant idea, and I was glad not to have to be trying to convince her it was in her best interest to get them to agree to a settlement so that she could take the money and run. Well. Limp, I guess.

She didn't seem to be running anywhere, I have to say. It was about this time that I began hearing, at a board meeting here, an aside there, that something was "wrong" with Margaret and it wasn't her knee. People had apparently been going out of their way to hold meetings when she could get there, or taking care of her knee for her once she had arrived. Meetings were planned as supper meetings, so she wouldn't have to cook. There was even a clean-up day at her house announced at one meeting I attended.

People in the community generally knew I was representing her, and for a while, I had been hearing words of real concern for Margaret. Then I began hearing rumors. She wasn't showing up at meetings. She had been out of control at one. She hadn't done what she said she was going to. There had been no follow-through. She'd dropped the ball.

Of course, I wasn't able to say anything specific in reply, but my general comments of "She's had a pretty tough time you know," were, for some reason, not being accepted anymore. I wasn't sure what was happening. Her doctor seemed to think she was mending, but what I was hearing was something else. People did not come to me now and ask "How's she feeling?" like they had in the first few months after the accident. It had seemed to me that many things had gone terribly wrong for Margaret for quite some time, but that was not information I could put out in general conversation. I could, however, talk with Audrey about it.

I decided to make sure nothing would stand in the way of my lunch with Audrey that week. We had had to cancel the last several lunches due to conflicting court schedules, which sometimes happened, but I needed her advice, and I made it clear to our secretary that we both needed to be free for lunch sometime that week. He looked at me, smiled his enigmatic smile and said, "Well, let's take a look."

Even after six years, I never knew if Philip was joking with me or not, if he liked me or not, if he even thought the least little bit about me at all, and frankly, it was such a relief not to have to worry about that. If I had known how wonderful it was to have a gay man as a secretary, I would have insisted on it through all those years of corporate law when good staff could make or break you, and I didn't have the least idea how to supervise anyone, let alone a woman who was older than I, straight, with two teen-aged daughters and a husband who went to mass with her every week.

I loved working with Philip. For a long time, I wanted him to like me. Then I got over myself, and it was fine, if a little disconcerting. He smiled his smile. I smiled my smile. He did his work. I did mine. We got along famously.

He was holding the book open on the desk, and I was trying to read the double schedule.

"Still getting used to your bifocals?" he said, noticing how I was bobbing my head.

"Yes," I said, stepping back so I could see him and noticing, for the first time, he wore them too.

"It won't take long," he murmured, but it was another of those moments for me when I realized consciously that not only was I becoming middle-aged, but so were most of the people around me, which comforted me somewhat. Only somewhat, but enough to brush the thought away.

There was time on Thursday, and I got him to red-line the hour. There was no use trying to go through Audrey to set up her own schedule, I reminded her when she met me at the Second Avenue Grill at noon.

"God, isn't it wonderful we can hire someone who can take care of us so well?" she beamed. "Now tell me, what's wrong with your client?" she continued as she unfolded her napkin, laid it in her lap, folded her hands together, and propped her chin up on them.

"Who says something is wrong with which client?" I asked, avoiding her eyes because I knew, of course, whom she was talking about.

"Oh come on," she said, impatiently looking around for the waiter.

"What do you know?" I asked, looking at the menu.

"Why are you reading that?" she answered. "You get the same thing every time."

"No, Audrey. *You* get the same thing every time. I get one of three different things." I smiled at her. She smiled back. We were friends again.

"Okay, ante up," I said. "What do you know?"

"Well, Barbara is having a dreadful time with her at the clinic. I'll have the chicken please, white meat only, and a Caesar salad, no anchovies."

The waiter turned to me. I quickly tried to remember: was this Wednesday? Was Brenna coming home for dinner? How much work did I have to do? Would I be coming home for dinner?

"Clams marinara on cappelini," I said after a long moment. Wednesday was her program night. Good. I could have one of my concoctions she felt was too disgusting to eat at the table. Sometimes I really loved being alone. Sometimes I couldn't believe I was 45 years old and still liked to have a dinner of graham crackers and milk in a blue bowl.

"And a small green salad to start," I finished. "Go on Audrey, get to the point."

"Nothing. That is the point. Barbara has finally got the board where she wants it. You know she's been working on that for months. Most of us will vote as a block for her now, all but two stubborn softball players who are old friends, apparently. Anyway, it seems clear Margaret wasn't really doing her work even before the accident, although since the accident she has not been in to the clinic at all. Barbara has been keeping tabs on her and trying to help, but it looks like she's just fallen apart, and you know the clinic isn't strong enough to hold that."

I watched, entranced, as she broke off a breadstick, section by section, popping each section in her mouth in turn, and continuing to use the breadstick as a pointer.

"So?" I asked.

"So for months, Barbara's been trying to ease her out, but Margaret wants an exit package that the clinic can't afford. It's come to the point where they can't wait around for her any longer, and I think they're going to have to get rid of her, somehow. It may get ugly, that's all. So I was wondering, how's the case coming along? Aren't you almost finished? How close to settling are you? It would be good if she had some cushion while she's rehab-ing. No one wants to throw her out in the street."

Well, Jesus H. Christ, I thought to myself. If this isn't the nastiest little piece of business I've ever watched Audrey Carr conduct. Margaret loved that clinic. If she lost it, well, I didn't really want to think about that.

"I'm surprised at you, Audrey," was all I could manage and felt angry it was all I could say.

"What do you mean?" she asked, genuinely taken aback. "Look, be reasonable. No one wants to hurt her. But that clinic is bigger than any one person. The institution has to survive, even if Margaret is not the person who's running it, which she hasn't been for quite some time, I gather. In a situation like this, Laura, things have to be taken care of, you know that."

"Then get someone else to take care of them," I said, carefully folding my napkin. "I suggest you get Barbara Chadwick to talk with Margaret directly about her exit package. I don't want to have anything to do with any of this, and I have nothing more to say about the matter. Will you excuse me?"

I got up from the table and left without waiting for an answer. I went out into the rain and walked down to the ferries and stood for a while. I felt as free as a scarf caught up and tossed by the wind. I really must be leaving. I had just told Audrey as much anyway. I felt sick to my stomach, but in an exciting way, the way I had at the roller coaster at the Connecticut state fair when I was a child. I can't tell you. I felt like a bird set free, headed for home. I was worried for Margaret, but I felt the best I had in months.

Instead of going back to the office, I went home that afternoon. Called Philip, told him I had gotten ill at lunch and had come home with a fever. Could he please? Certainly. Any messages? None.

Good. I sat in my chair by the window, got out my solitaire deck, and began thinking about Margaret. If I could just get her to keep her mouth shut, if I could just explain to her that we were very, very close to getting a settlement, there would be peace, if not milk and honey, on the other side. I planned. I practiced. I talked to the crows outside the window. I hoped.

I called her. We talked. When we went into the mediation, she gave me a thumbs up and then put her index finger and her thumb together and made as though she were zipping her mouth closed. I didn't probe. I didn't ask. I just made sure I had all my papers together.

It wasn't such a bad mediation, as far as those things go. Opposing counsel said the same kinds of things they had said during the depo, except a little more aggressively. Brice was there, drumming his fingernails, which for some reason, I had begun to find amusing. Buffed and shined fingernails. I decided he could afford it, and if he wanted to do it, why not? The mediator was an older man I had worked with some before and had generally felt to be reasonable, if not overly bright. I had to object to the weight issue three times before he would let it drop, finally deciding it could rest under the thin-skull rule.

Oh, it was an actual case, kind of interesting. The rule generally holds that if you toss a brick out the window, and it hits someone in the head, and that someone has had a previous skull injury and so is weak in that spot, if the brick kills that person, you are still responsible, even though the brick would not have killed an ordinary person. It was not exactly the kind of liberation speech that I think Margaret wanted, but it worked. I was not there to make a political statement about Margaret's size. Brenna is nearly as big as Margaret; personally, as I have already said, I find large women attractive. I didn't know, and I didn't care if the mediator did. I wanted to get Margaret her money, not change the world.

I could see her tense up as the afternoon went on, but I only hoped she would keep herself buttoned tight. My cross-examination of Brice was simple, but effective. "But you did strike her with your car, did you not? You did hit her, is that correct?" That sort of thing.

It really was a pretty simple case. They did not, as threatened, bring in a report from an accident specialist which meant they didn't have one. It was just another legal bluff. Margaret had parked so close to the crosswalk, any estimate would have been statistically insignificant anyway. He should have been going so slowly that even if she did walk out in front of his car, he would have already been stopped for the crosswalk.

The mediator seemed to agree. We came to a close. I felt

confident about approaching the opposing counsel in the hall to make a settlement offer. If they went for it, great. They really didn't have too much to stand on. If they didn't, they could make a counter-offer, or we would wait a while, see if they would come to their senses.

I approached the insurance company attorney, having decided to ignore the other one since she hadn't spoken to me once or even made written contact about filing a counter-suit. At least that much was smart on their part. My offer was in the high range, but not out of the question, given Margaret's length of treatment and difficulties.

"Out of the question," the insurance attorney answered, without even consulting his colleague. He was, however, prepared to make a counter-offer which was about half what I had suggested. This was fairly typical and did not distress me. Let them stew in it awhile, I thought.

"I'll consult with my client," I said. I walked over to the reception area where Margaret was madly turning the pages of an old magazine. I named the figure and tried to explain the positioning that was going on, but before I could get the words out of my mouth, she heaved herself up from the sofa, took her cane, and walked out without a word.

"We'll think about it," I said back to counsel. "I'll confer further with my client, and I'll get back to you. My client had another engagement she was late for," I offered by way of explanation and gathered my things.

This time, he shook my hand. We were on our way. But where the hell was Margaret? In that moment, I found myself thinking that I liked her a little better when she couldn't get around quite so much. I decided to let the matter rest for a few days until she calmed down. Representing Margaret, I thought then, was sort of like learning to live with the weather in Seattle: if you didn't like it one moment, all you needed to do was wait; it would change in a moment. Things were going to be all right, I thought as I drove home. At least, we were in the same ballpark for a settlement. We would dicker back and forth. Margaret would get a reasonable amount of money, not what she wanted, but more than she had. I would get paid and get to go home. I felt I had done a good day's work.

Summer in the City

Margaret

One thing I do know: all this would have been very different if I hadn't fallen and ended up in the hospital for three more days. And I never would have fallen if my knee hadn't already been in bad shape from Brice's criminal driving skills. I never did things like fall in the shower. I'm a big woman, but I've never been clumsy like that. I've been athletic every day of my life. I mean, I used to be. I played baseball, the usual kid things, until the accident, and then I was in the hospital, in and out for most of the next two years, but after that, I really got into golf. I had a great, powerful drive. I could hit four hundred yards, easy.

I played every weekend through my teens and until I got into college. Once I got into college, everything changed. I don't suppose you can call marching at political rallies athletic, although I do recall there were some times with the cops in

Berkeley, running away from the tear gas that required just about every bit of stamina that I had.

But I danced. I always danced. I used to dance with Duke. He was the one who taught me how to Lindy. Not that I could do that now, but I always danced. Before Brice hit me, I had been going to an African dance class where they didn't care what size you were, none of this anorectic ballet stuff. I loved that class. I went religiously, every Saturday morning. What a lifesaver that was, completely revitalized me every week.

And I want to tell you, no matter what anyone says, I was in good shape before Brice hit me, and all things considered I was even in pretty good shape before I fell. But I know this: I wouldn't have fallen if I hadn't already been weak in that knee. I mean, I was getting around. It wasn't there yet, but the knee was on its way to full strength. Sure, it hurt some of the time, but that was hardly an issue anymore. Thanks to Kore, I really had done well with my rehab.

But I want you to write this down. My size had nothing, nothing to do with my fall—or getting hit by Brice. If my size was such a big issue, it seems like he would have seen me coming. I mean, his attorneys made me sound like a beached whale when they were talking about future medical needs, and if that Slattery woman wasn't bulimic, I'll eat my cane.

Well, I fell is what happened, that's all. It wasn't such a big deal, or at least it wouldn't have been if I hadn't already been crippled by Brice. I slipped getting into the shower, and I landed right on it.

By the time I got my clothes on enough to get to the doctor, Kore was so worried she wanted to call an ambulance for me. The knee had swollen so much I couldn't get the brace around it. I called my doctor, and she wasn't in yet, thank you very much. Finally, Kore made them page her, and when we eventually got through to her in the operating room, she told Kore to take me directly to emergency, which I must admit, scared the hell out of both Kore and me, but we went.

Well, I was in surgery within six hours. I never left the hospital. They took me right up to the surgery prep area, and I waited there with Kore until an operating room was free.

After surgery, my doctor told Kore that the bone in my leg was so soft from all the antibiotics I had taken that when I landed on it, I just "blew it out," which is a technical term for saying there was nothing much left of all the work I had been doing for the last eight months. All the previous surgery to reconstruct the tibial plateau was destroyed.

She patched me back together, but I had to stay in the hospital for a couple more days and nights. I was in and out of consciousness; I know Kore stayed with me the whole time, at least she told me she did. I remember being alone though, and other times I remember hearing my doctor talking to the nurses late at night. One night I remember her yelling at them out in the hall for giving me so many pain meds, saying I was sucking up meds through the I.V. like it was champagne, like I had something to do with it.

And then one of the nurses said, "But her drain, she's bleeding like a pig, don't you think she's in a lot of pain?" And then, mercifully, Kore got up and shut the door and combed my hair with her fingers while I cried and begged her to take me home.

That's really all I wanted—to go home. The dreams I was having in the hospital—I'm sure it was the drugs—were the worst I'd ever had. They were all a jumble—with Roger and Duke and penises and shriveled legs. They were horrid, just horrid. The pain was so much more intense the second time. I just wanted to die. I felt like my knee wasn't mine anymore—like it was, but it wasn't—and I couldn't do anything to make it be mine ever again.

They wanted to put in an artificial knee, but they were worried because of the infection from before. An artificial knee only lasts ten years anyway. And they can only do the operation twice; then they have to fuse your knee, and you have no movement at all. I'm fifty now. You do the math.

I've often wondered what would have happened about this if I'd have gone through with a trial. Would I have gotten more for my future medical care which I'm definitely going to need? And I've wondered, God I've laid in bed wondering for more nights than I can count, I've wondered what would have happened if I hadn't given in to Laura and settled the case with a trial.

My doctor had submitted a report for the mediation that my knee was permanent and stationary at that time and that she expected a full recovery. Of course, that was then. I know, in fact she told me, she would have testified completely differently after my fall. Well, it's all water under the bridge now.

I did what I did. I got some bad advice, and I acted on it. It all happened so fast; I hate how they want you to make a decision that will affect the whole rest of your life, and there isn't much you can find out—well, it's a crap shoot. That's what Duke always said, and it's true, it's still true today.

No, I am not going to talk with you about how much money I ended up with. Why should I? What will you make of dollar amounts? What do dollar amounts mean to you anyway or any of your readers? Do they know what my medical expenses were? Do they know my attorney wanted thirty-three percent to go to trial? Now there's a real number to think about. They tell me that's standard. She gets thirty-three percent of my future earnings. Not a bad racket; nice work if you can get it, I suppose, or if you can stomach it.

Anyway, what if I were to tell you what I got. What would it do for you? What would it satisfy in you? That I got enough? That I got justice?

Look at my leg, and tell me where there is justice. My leg is permanently crooked. The scars on my legs, both of them now, will never go away. I can't walk without a limp and a cane now, and I never will be able to again. I can't walk all over town like

I used to. I can't do the Seward Park loop ever again. I can't make love the way I used to. I can't do anything the way I used to. I'm fifty years old, and my leg is permanently damaged. They could have given me $100,000, which they didn't, and it wouldn't have made up for my leg.

And if I hadn't gone to work for the city, I can tell you I wouldn't even be able to get health insurance. I had to go somewhere big, somewhere I could be absorbed by the group because I had to have insurance on my knee, and I knew—well, I'd already been turned down for an individual policy.

Okay, I ended up with forty thousand dollars. Would you like to know how much a total knee replacement costs, the one I'm going to need in seven more years? Just about that much. I didn't get enough to go back to school and get some formal training, so that I could secure a better job. Contrary to what you've heard, not only did I not get enough to never work again, I didn't even get enough to take any time but the absolute minimum I needed to get my leg well enough to walk on. It took me four months of hard, hard work to learn to walk again, after not being able to walk on it for almost a year and a half without crutches. Are you getting the picture? Look at it this way: I didn't make as much as Annie Bartleby skimmed the clinic.

My attorney took her cut off the top, the doctor, insurance company, and my physical therapist took the rest. What do you think now? Do you think that's enough money for my knee?

Brice did. He thought he'd been totally ripped off. He told me so. I was speechless when he spoke to me before his lawyers hustled him away. But what do you want me to say about this? I used the money for a down payment on the house Kore and I live in, a little house, a tiny little house in Fremont, in the fringe area with all the rest of the lesbians who don't get paid what they are worth. We don't buy houses on Capital Hill or in Bellevue or in Greenlake with the rest of the middle-class folks. No, we live in Fremont, hardly even a proper neighborhood, further from downtown than Mercer Island, because that's all we can afford. And I only hope, when I need another operation, I'll have put enough in the house, so that I can get a home equity loan to cover my needs.

That's what I got from Dr. Harry Brice and from Laura Gilbert. That's what I got for months of hell and years of pain. That's what I got for crossing the street one day in broad daylight.

That's what I got. Are you satisfied now? Do you think your readers will sit there and say, "Well, that seems like a lot of money to me." Let me tell you, it's not Harry Brice's take-home pay for one fucking month. Don't kid yourself. There is a system in this country, and it doesn't work for women like you and me. It doesn't work for people like us at all; it never has and it never will.

There is nothing that can be done for me now. Something happened, and it can't be fixed. All we can do is go forward. The past is past. And some things will never get better.

Oh, I know I'm not supposed to say all that. After the fall, when I was having such bad nightmares and in so much pain, I did talk to a therapist a couple of times, but frankly, it was pretty useless. I only saw her because Kore and the doctor really put the screws to me.

I went, but so? I mean, it wasn't like anything could be done about any of it. She kept wanting me to talk about Duke, but it was so different. What happened with Duke was nothing like what happened with Brice. That happened in July. We were coming home from a baseball game, Duke and me, and it was raining the way it does in July in Olympia, but it hadn't been raining in Tacoma, where we'd gone. Gosh, we had a great time that day. I guess the shrink thought some of that was coming up, which was ridiculous.

She wasn't listening very well. I never dream about Duke, except for sometimes. And when I do, they are happy dreams. I like having dreams about Duke because even if it's a bad dream, once Duke comes, I get rescued. I could be in the worst predicament—and boy, I do have some dreams with pretty weird stuff going on in them—but if Duke comes in, that's it. I know I'm going to be okay. There is one kind of dream where he comes. . . . And we start flying, and then everything gets dark as a rainstorm in winter, and I wake up screaming. But I almost never have that dream, not anymore.

Mostly, when I dream of Duke, I know everything will be all right. In fact, I wished I had those dreams more often. I wished I had them as often as I have the other dreams. And this therapist, when I finally got her to listen to the other dreams, well, she just couldn't get off of them. My God, it was this and that, and finally she came right out and said I was having post-traumatic stress syndrome, that the dreams were really memories, repressed memories of abuse.

Well, I can tell you, I remember the first day she said that very well. I had been in session with her, telling her about a dream I'd had about Claudia, when all of a sudden I got very, very cold. And my head felt like something was trying to get out so badly, I thought it would burst open, literally, right there in the room. And I wasn't able to talk to her anymore, and I started to shake. And she kept saying, what's happening, what's happening, and all I could see, like it was a movie going on inside my eyelids, all I could see was the dream I kept having about Roger, and I guess I started to moan and rock myself, which is what I do when I have that dream.

It was a little embarrassing to do that in front of her. But you know, I had liked her up until then. She reminded me somehow of Doc Lennox before he became the torture expert after the accident. Before that, he was Duke's and my doctor, and he was very kind to me. There was something about the way the therapist sat or tilted her head or something, I don't know. But when she started in on me like I was a very little child, talking to me like she didn't think I could hear her, which

I could, perfectly well, and she kept on asking me what I saw, so finally I told her. And I was crying and stuff, because that dream always scares me, but then she started in on how it's not a dream, it's a memory, and I'm telling you, I just about puked my way out of the office.

I mean, I think I know what is real or not. She had me going there for a little while, but the more I thought about it, the more I just didn't believe it. I had a perfectly normal childhood except that my dad died. There are lots of people out there who go through that kind of thing. It's just not a big deal. So I was sad; that's okay. Plenty of people get sad. It's no big deal, and I didn't appreciate her making it a bigger deal than it was.

Well, I just didn't believe her. I know what happened to me, and I know that I had a very, very active imagination as a child. Claudia was always saying so, and I know nothing like that ever happened. It was me. It was just me.

And frankly, I think falling made me remember not being able to do what I wanted, feeling really vulnerable after Duke's accident, and not being able to be in control of my life after my mother married Roger. I mean, I never liked Roger, but I think I would have remembered something that big. I was there, after all, and the therapist wasn't.

What I decided was that she just wanted me to continue in therapy, for her own needs, specifically monetary. I was getting ready to terminate with her at that point, and I think she knew it. I think she was just trying to latch on to whatever she could to keep me there. And what happened in the office wasn't all that unusual for me. It didn't usually happen in the day, but it happened often enough at night for me to know it was just a dream, just a bad dream.

Honestly, I think I knew better than she did, and better than she ever could have known, what had happened to me. I didn't particularly appreciate being told that I didn't. So I left her, and I didn't go back. The dreams cleared up when I stopped taking the pain medicine, so I guess we know the answer to that problem.

Well, it was funny. My knee hurt for a really long time, and I was taking a lot of meds. It was kind of getting in the way of my life; I mean I wasn't able to do anything. So I had started going to an acupuncturist for some headaches I was having, and she told me she could treat me better if I wasn't taking them, so one day, I just stopped. Probably wasn't the smartest thing I'd ever done. I had the shakes and everything, but it's better now.

I mean, I still have a lot of pain sometimes, but if I can't get in to see Teresa, my acupuncturist, I just take some over-the-counter stuff and get some rest, and I'm fine until she can see me. The sharp, aching pain comes at night, just like the dreams. But it goes away during the day. I think the pain is probably because the leg is still so weak. If I didn't have to use it so much, it probably wouldn't hurt so much.

You know, I talked about all the dreams and stuff with Teresa at the time. She helped me as much as anyone, especially with the pain. But she listened to me, too, listened to me talk about Duke and how much I missed him. Do you believe in cellular memory? Teresa does, says all acupuncturists do. She says the reason I had so many bad dreams in the hospital was from the first accident, an anniversary kind of thing. I like her, and I feel better after I've been to see her. She has some stuff that I rub on my leg to make it feel better—sometimes I get this pins-and-needles sensation down there, and it just drives me wild. Anyway, I like her, but sometimes I think acupuncturists are just as full of bullshit as the regular doctors are, only a different kind, you know what I mean?

I don't know. I was hit by a car. Then, just as I was getting better, I fell. My life changed. Things happen. Life goes on and mostly nothing changes, but when it does, there really isn't much you can do about it. That's what the lawsuit and therapy taught me. You might as well just go on because there isn't much that can be done. All that effort, all that pain around the lawsuit, all that humiliation, the insults and insinuations . . . I'll tell you what, next time, I'm just leaving with my pride intact. They wouldn't know what justice was any more than that shrink knew what the truth was. They just don't know.

Laura

You know enough by now to know that things aren't ever as simple as we hope. Couldn't have been anyway, given the personalities involved, with either Audrey or Margaret. I walked into work on Monday actually feeling refreshed. I'd had a relaxing weekend, one of the first in many months; I got out the kayak and began working on getting it ready for a trip. When I got to the office on Monday, I didn't know what my schedule was or what I was doing. I couldn't even remember the last time that had happened.

I walked in, tried to make small talk with Philip, the little he would allow, then asked to see the schedule book and saw that lunch had been red-lined. I pointed to it, asked "Audrey?" and he nodded.

I took my morning latte back to my office and turned to face the window behind my desk. The office suite I shared with Audrey was near the court house, which was great, and near the edge of downtown, which was even better. There were a number of truly wonderful old brick buildings facing my window. Audrey had views of the Sound, but I preferred watching the people on the streets below, and I found looking at the old Romanesque arches very comforting.

No appointments until eleven, a letter to write, ten calls to return: I had time to think. Of course, I never should have gotten up and left the table at lunch with Audrey. Tactically, it left me wide open. But somehow, I didn't particularly care anymore.

You can call it a midlife crisis if you want, but something had happened to me. I think there just comes a point, if you're lucky, when you stop caring whether or not someone, anyone, likes you, and you begin to wonder if you actually like yourself. The answer to that question may be yes or no, but if you are being honest with yourself about the question, the answer is never easy.

Let's be clear, I had wanted Audrey to like me. I wanted to be a part of the community. I wanted to know what was going on. I wanted to be "inside." It wasn't like I was ever going to be in with the twenty-year-old crowd (that's how small Seattle is), but I wanted to belong somewhere. I really did. I came here broken and alone, after years of being in the thick of things in D.C., and I appreciated being sought out and included by someone like Audrey. For six years, I wanted it enough to be outside myself. And then, one day, it wasn't enough anymore.

I had been sitting at the Friends Meeting, like I did most Sundays, trying not to listen to the same people who talked every Sunday and made you want to go up to them and say, "What, exactly, moves you to speak every single week, and do you think you could cut it a little short?" which was extremely unQuakerly, but then I wasn't raised a Quaker. I'm still sort of new at it after six years. I still missed hymn music. I even missed pew seats. I must admit I never would have thought I would miss the hard, intentionally uncomfortable, Congregational pews, but I did.

In any event, I was there in my hard, uncomfortable folding chair, and I was waiting for the Spirit to fill me and see if it moved me to speak, which it never had, and I hoped to God never would, when suddenly the lullaby oboe line from *First Gymnopedie* broke through the chatter in my head, and I began to weep. I got up, walked out, drove down to the lake, and sat on the sea wall, watching the line of clouds advance from the south and pass me by, an unbroken, but always changing progression in which I often took comfort.

This was not the first time, certainly, that I had to leave the Meeting in tears. The first year I was here, I couldn't even bring myself to go to the Congregational Church, my grief was so strong. Over the years, I came to appreciate the Quaker approach to all things, but I still missed the music. I missed my home.

I missed my child. You can tell me she wasn't mine, but it won't matter. I don't much care what you or anyone else has to say about this anymore. I raised a child. She was as much mine as if she had come from me. She was taken from me, and I walked away because I believed it to be better for her.

Or maybe it wasn't even that. I can bear the scrutiny of cynics now. Maybe it was that I couldn't stand the pain of seeing her and not being able to be with her, not being a part of her life anymore. Maybe I walked away because it was better for me; to stay, in such a limited way I didn't even know what she was doing in school, was so excruciating I couldn't bear it.

Because I had never considered her a territory of mine, not a possession. It had never occurred to me that someone who loved Amanda would actually ever take her away from someone else who so obviously loved her. But maybe that's because I wasn't a biological mother: I didn't see her as a territory because she didn't come from my body. Maybe I don't really understand.

But there are some things I do understand. I understand that children need love and attention. I understand that children are their own territories, and that they have the right to form attachments with whomever they will. What Rebecca understood her relationship to be with Amanda precluded Amanda's relationship with me, her rights as mother seemed to negate whatever rights I had as a parent, because I wasn't a man. Can there really only be one mother? What did I have with Amanda then? Was my grief not as real, even though no one would sanctify my tears? Is loss less when unsanctified?

I had waited years for someone able to hear my anguish

and to absolve my guilt. Brenna heard, and Nettie and I began to wonder for whom was I waiting? I didn't know, but what became clear was that if I kept on waiting, I might be waiting still. Some things you get over and let go of; some you live with. I was beginning to understand this grief was something I would carry with me to my grave; that alone was sanctification.

I knew, that afternoon sitting there, that at least I could be clean about it. I had done what I had done. No one forced me. I did the best I could, took my best shot. I had lost. I remember arguing with Rebecca when she was first thinking about having a child, saying, "Who will feed her when you're on rounds? Who will hold her in the night when you're in the operating room?"

And at the time, I told her it wouldn't be me. I didn't want to have a child. I was too afraid. Afraid I couldn't do it right; afraid I shouldn't be a parent at all. But Amanda changed all that. By the Grace of whatever little Godforce she had inside her, she changed all that.

And I changed, too. By loving her in the newness of her life, I came to believe that I had the right to have a life, too. I never dreamed that I would have to give her up to have that. But that day on the sea wall, I realized that I wasn't going to give my life away again, that life I had paid for with Amanda, with every night I wake up in the middle of the night still, thinking I have heard her cry out for me. I wouldn't give my life to her mother then, and I certainly wasn't going to give it to whatever Audrey Carr or anyone else was charging for membership into the club.

I had ransomed my own life. I had paid plenty for it, more than I knew I had. I didn't need Audrey Carr to tell me I was okay anymore or to try to do what I thought was expected of a good, community-fearing lesbian attorney anymore. I had my life, what there was left of it, and I was going to spend it where I chose, counting every day like a dime, not a down payment for tomorrow, but on this hour, this day. My life as an attorney, and possibly as Audrey Carr's friend, was over.

And I was finally ready to say so. I decided, why wait? Monday is a good day to start things. I decided lunch was going to serve as the backdrop, and I felt like a king. My stepson Joe told me once I couldn't be a king, that only boys could be king. He was so wrong. "King" is a feeling; you may have to fight for it, but anyone can have it.

And maybe because of that feeling, lunch was easy. For once, Audrey was speechless, but covered herself by saying she was not surprised. That said, there really wasn't much to talk about. It was one of the first times I had seen Audrey box herself into a corner. I quite enjoyed myself, had something entirely new on the menu. I would be gone as soon as I could wrap up the few cases I had left. Philip could forward my mail.

"What will you do?" she said at one point, delicately playing with the bone of the remains of her chicken.

"I honestly don't know," I answered, supremely satisfied. I had finally realized I had to close one door before another could open. Not knowing felt like an achievement to me.

"Well, it's been quite a ride," she said.

I just smiled at her. I did not think, from her tone, that we would be friends later. I was not sure that would be a tragedy. She left abruptly, pleading court time, and I paid the bill and sauntered back to the office.

Not to be outdone, perhaps I should have expected this, there was a message from Margaret waiting for me when I got back from lunch. Well, why not? I thought. There wasn't anything that was going to break my mood that day.

Not even when Margaret announced she had to see me that afternoon. "Fine," I said and meant it. Go for double treys as Joe would say in NBA-ese.

She was in the reception area within the hour. When I walked out to get her, I could see the steam rising off her. If her anger could have come out of her hands, she would have torched the magazine she was holding. Well, I thought, no time like the present.

I followed her painful progress down the hall. She seemed much worse than on Friday, but maybe it was just her anger. I never really knew.

I took her into my office and instead of sitting behind my desk, I motioned for her to take one of the armchairs and brought my pad over to sit with her, conversationally, in the other. I offered her a drink of water. I offered her the coffee table for her leg. She declined both and continued to stare out the window. I waited. There is nothing like a long silence for effect.

Finally, she began to speak, and her voice was so low I had to lean toward her to hear.

"I trusted you," she began. "I trusted this mediation was something that would work in my favor, as you had told me. I am paying you to guide me, to take me through the ins and outs of a complex legal procedure."

Boy, she's practiced this, I thought, while keeping my face concerned and open.

"You have betrayed me," she said, so softly I almost didn't hear her.

"Could we slow this down, just a little?" I asked. "Could we please start at the beginning?"

She brought her hand down on the side of the chair so hard, I was afraid she had hurt herself, but when she finally looked at me, I realized she wasn't feeling anything but anger. And then I began to become a little afraid myself.

"Margaret, please go slowly with me and explain this," I pleaded with her. "Help me understand. I was under the impression you were going to think about the offer. If you don't like it, we don't have to do anything. We can take this thing all the way to a jury trial if you'd like. I think we might win. You never know, but if you feel this strongly, we can try. Listen. I'm your attorney. You hired me. I work for you. You tell me what you want me to do, and I'll do it."

Which I have been doing all along, I thought to myself. She clearly thought she would have made the better lawyer than me. There were always clients who liked to direct their own cases and clients who accept direction, who come to you because they think you know more than they. The majority of folks are in the latter category; Margaret, of course, was in the first. I thought, well, if she accepted the settlement money, she could go to law school herself. I knew of an office that had space for a new tenant.

I had to stop myself then, before any of that showed on my face. I let the silence fill in as before. Light came in the west windows and floated down in between us. I just waited.

"I don't know what to do," she said, spitting the words out one by one as though they were teeth. Well, why didn't you tell me? I thought. Now we can get to the root of the problem.

"You've told me before about accepting. You've told me before I won't get more if I take it to trial, only you will get more."

She cut her eyes around to me again. I kept my face chess-nonchalant.

"There is a chance of that, Margaret. I wouldn't be doing a very good job as your attorney if I didn't tell you that. You have a chance to lose it all. You have a chance to get more. It's a gamble."

"I don't like gambles. I got hit by a car. And all you've been able to get for me is not even going to cover my fucking medical bills. You tell me what I'm supposed to do about it. I am paying you for *something*, am I not?"

Well, you aren't paying me enough to take this, I thought, and then remembered lunch. Four more cases, I thought. Four more cases.

"Margaret, it was just an offer. They are trying to position themselves, trying to get the best deal they can. We don't have to answer them at all if you don't like it. We can just go to the next step of taking it to trial."

"You've already said that. You know very well I can't gamble with this leg. I don't have any reserve. I have nothing to fall back on. I'm not some rich doctor's daughter. I can't take the hit, and you know it, so stop with this bullshit."

"Actually," I said very slowly, not rising to the bait, keeping my voice low, too, but softer, trying to help her remember some semblance of reasonable conversation, "Margaret, I don't know what your personal financial situation is, and I don't want to know. But if you don't feel like you can risk going to trial, let's make them a counter-offer. We'll keep negotiating until we get a figure you can live with. I promise you that you won't have to settle for their low-ball offer. He's just marking his territory, like any dog."

I had hoped the scatological reference would make her smile, and it did.

"We get another chance?"

"We get as many chances as you need. We're not going to settle this until you're ready."

"How much more do you think?"

"I think the mediator will recommend at least ten grand more, and whatever he recommends will help our position."

"Ten grand! That's almost as insulting!" she shouted.

I waited until the sound died away.

"Margaret," I began and then faded away until she looked at me. "Margaret, nothing is going to be enough for what you've gone through."

She looked as though I had struck her, and I wondered for a moment if she would cry, but she caught herself. I could almost see her getting a grip on her breathing and facial muscles.

"Nothing is going to make up for what you've been through, and I never promised you that, did I?"

Like a truculent child, she shook her head.

"But we are going to get you something. Not enough. But more than you have. And enough to cover your expenses and maybe enough to put away for a house or so you don't have to work for quite a long time, if you need that."

She shook her head like a fish caught on a hook and turned her head back to the window. This time, I was quite certain she was crying. I got up and brought her the box of tissue I kept in my bottom drawer for my own tears.

"I know this isn't easy. I understand your anger." This much I had said to clients a thousand times if I had said it once, but I still really meant it.

"There isn't enough I can get for you to make you well again. You're going to have to do that yourself. So take some time. Think about what you would like me to counter-offer. We'll wait a week for the mediator, and then we'll decide, okay?"

She nodded, still looking away, and brought the tissue up to wipe her eyes.

"It's not fair," she said, muffled.

"No, it isn't," I said. "It never is. We just have to do the best we can with what we have.

"When was the last time you got any sleep?" I said on a hunch. She certainly looked like a madwoman, like she hadn't slept in weeks. For some reason, I hadn't noticed it at the depo, maybe the lights, maybe my concentration was elsewhere, whatever. She looked terrible.

"Last July," she whispered.

"Try to get some, will you? It's hard to make a good decision when you're sleep-deprived. Take some time this week to just rest and think about what you want to do."

"I haven't been doing anything else," she said, looking over her shoulder at me and then back out the window.

"Well, then get Kore to take you out for dinner or something special and stop thinking about it," I said in what I hoped was a joking tone and got up to let her know the visit was over.

She made me wait for a moment, then pushed herself upright.

"Okay," she said. "I'm sorry. I've been having a hard time."

"Yes, you have," I said, opening the office door and standing in the hallway so that she would go toward the exit door. "You've had about the toughest time of anyone I know. And you hardly deserved it."

"Thanks for your kindness," she said and squeezed my hand as she went out. "I'll be in touch," she added, as she limped down the hall.

I watched her go. She was right. It wasn't fair. I went back in my office, closed the door and slumped in my chair, looking out the window again. Life wasn't fair, was the thing of it. Still, we went on and made the best of it. I still believed in making the best of it. Maybe it's the Yankee in me. Maybe it's the Amanda in me. Maybe it was that I did think we could get her ten grand and maybe more. It would be enough to buy her something, maybe even a few nights' rest. What a crummy job I had gotten myself into.

I swung back to my desk and went back to work. No use wasting a perfectly good afternoon. All I could do for the moment for Margaret was wait.

Lammas

Margaret

So just let me ask you this: if it were true that the board asked me to resign after my last surgery, if that were true, how come, not two months later, they asked me to come back?

Sure they did. I bet none of your other interviewees told you that, did they? Well, they did. I was asked to come back to a board meeting—actually there were several board members who asked me during the course of that meeting. There are people you could ask. Why don't you ask Barbara Chadwick? She was there.

Or let me ask you something else: if they asked me to resign, why did they have that fundraising dinner in my honor? If they asked me to resign, why honor me later? You never would have met me if they'd asked me to resign because there never would have been any fundraising dinner for you to see me.

This is not hard to figure out. I resigned. Didn't you just

hear me tell you what life was like after my surgeries? After I fell in the shower, I couldn't have come to work if I had wanted to. I was out on disability and had been for several months, anyway. I was still working, of course, as much as I could, but I had gotten away from the day-to-day thing, and they were doing fine. I mean, they needed someone there every day; they needed an administrator. The clinic couldn't really function, not well, and not for any prolonged period of time without one because the clinic had gotten so big and so busy, but it couldn't be me. Not at that point in time. I just couldn't do it.

So I resigned. It was the right thing to do. I needed to step aside, so they could get someone full-time, someone who could take the place to the next level. I could have done it if I had been healthy, but I wasn't. And I knew I wasn't going to be one hundred percent for a long time. So, really, the only right thing to do was to leave. I gave my resignation at the first board meeting I could get to after that last big surgery.

Of course, I remember it. I've remembered all of this so far, haven't I? What do you want me to tell you?

Okay. There was a board meeting. Like I've already told you, it was after the mediation. I went specifically to resign. Barbara and I had worked out a plan we thought the board would accept finally. It was basically a done deal that night. All we needed was board approval, and by that time, Barbara was president of the board, so we weren't worried about anything. Together, we had expanded the membership quite a bit from six to twenty members, and they were all in agreement by then.

Well, after we discovered the embezzlement, it just became very clear to us that we didn't have the resources we needed from a board to make sure the clinic would survive. Up to that point, the board had been quite small, just the first doctors who had been there in the beginning, the ones who hired me actually, and some of the very early volunteers. We'd all been working together for a very long time, and when Barbara pointed that out, and I realized how polarized the board had become with the anger over Annie's betrayal, I knew we just couldn't go on like that. The clinic had just gotten too big for one small family. We really needed professionals on the board. I completely agreed with Barbara on that point.

So Barbara and I sat down one afternoon and figured out who we needed, which skills we needed and what holes we needed plugged, and who we knew we might be able to get. We went to the old board with that and just sold them on each position. As soon as they realized how bad the situation was, and what we needed to do, it wasn't a problem. Many of them resigned shortly thereafter, anyway. I think we all just got pretty burnt out, to tell you the truth. God knows, I was tired.

And again, I want you to understand what it was like for us to know that Annie had stolen from us all. I mean, we had worked, all of us on the board, like dogs to get that place going. And to think that Annie had taken the money was more than some of the women could handle. It was so sad.

And it was very, very difficult. Having to go to them and say, week after week . . . At that point, when I first discovered there was a problem, and I couldn't be there every day to run the clinic, we were having weekly board meetings at my house, to try to figure out how to keep going. It was hell having to say to them every week how sorry I was that I hadn't been more careful, that I hadn't watched her, that I didn't know, that even if she had been my lover, I never should have . . . well, it doesn't matter now. It was humiliating, and I guess some of those women got tired of hearing it, too, because soon after we expanded the board, they left.

So Barbara and I just kept asking women we knew who could add the skills we needed. Just ordinary board kind of skills—you know the old adage—wisdom, wealth, or work; you either give money or professional guidance, whatever your field is, or you strengthen the organization by work. Fundraising or marketing or outreach to certain communities, that sort of thing. So we added an attorney, Audrey Carr, and we added another accountant to help out with the books, and we added some health care professionals to help us with outreach, a nurse named Bernice Johnson, who was very active in the women's athletic community and could bring in lots of sports injuries (most of those women have private insurance, which we desperately needed for operating funds), and we added a physical therapist for referrals, that sort of thing.

We added some rich women Barbara knew, too. And I'm not going to tell you who they are because I don't think that's anyone's business. They get hit on enough for money. I don't think it's fair to publicize their names. The point is, we added a lot of women who could really help us during that time. If it weren't for some very large donations, I can tell you right now, that clinic would not have survived one year after Annie Bartleby. They were all strong women, either Barbara or I knew each one of them, and together we made a good working team.

And not once, I'm telling you, not once did someone come to me and say, we want you to resign. In fact, that last meeting where I was officially still the administrator, although on leave, that last meeting which was actually the first meeting I went to after my second reconstruction from when I fell, they were all so nice to me.

Everyone was worried about me, and they asked how I was and generally made me feel very comfortable. And when I said I just couldn't go on, they were great about it. They were all very kind about my work, how loyal I had been, and how hard I had tried, and how much they appreciated all my work, that sort of thing.

There were some women there I didn't know too much, and I never liked that physical therapist very well; there was something about her that was a little butch for my blood. I know I'm not supposed to say that anymore, but I never liked her, and frankly, I was kind of insulted by the way she acted when I first came to the board with the embezzlement—like she didn't believe me and wanted to see for herself, but I guess she did, because I didn't hear any more about it.

Anyway, it was a new board, and I never worked as closely with them as I had with the old board. There were some of them I hardly knew at all. That last year, well, I've described to you how it was. But Barbara knew them all, and it was a good board. They had things well in hand, and, as Barbara said, it was time for me to leave, it really was.

Sure it made me sad. When Barbara first suggested it, when I was convalescing after the plate surgery, it made me a little angry, to tell you the truth. But mostly, it made me sad, really sad. Still, Barbara was right, and it didn't take me very long to see that. She would stop by once or twice a month, like she had in the beginning, although this time she didn't bring the books. We'd gotten someone to take that over, thank God, and we'd just sit there in the old apartment and wait for the rain to stop, and we'd talk.

Oh, about everything. Gossip about the clinic, which I really missed, and what needed to be done, and who could we get to do it, and who was sleeping with whom, that sort of thing. We talked about a lot of things.

Well, sure I was lonely. All day by myself—Kore had graduated and become a full-time R.N., which was great because we really needed the money. I was a little worried about her after she moved in with me, and she was getting paid to take care of me—I wasn't worried because she wasn't earning her pay. God knows she was, but I was worried that it might look bad. You know, people might think there was some kind of financial impropriety there, I don't know. But there wasn't. Anyway, she'd graduated and was working full time, and she was happy when she came home from work and that made me happy. But I was lonely all by myself all day. Too much time to think. I never do well with too much time to think. I brood. It's the Irish in me.

But face it, I had lost everything. I had lost my previous

relationship, my clinic, and the use of my knee. As Barbara pointed out, I had gained some things too: Kore was quite a gain over Annie, and she's never stolen from me yet! But I lost a lot that year. I lost a lot. And I had a lot of time to think about how much I had lost, and why I had lost it, and how unfair it was. It was so unfair.

Duke used to say, "Well, honey, life's just a horse race," and I thought about that, and I wondered if he really believed that. He'd get up from a losing race, and he'd tear his betting ticket stubs and let them flutter to the ground under the stands like they were confetti, and he'd laugh, and we'd go out to the parking lot and turn the radio up really loud and sing all the way home. I wished I could do that. I tried.

But I deserved better, godammit. I did. I worked my ass off for that clinic, and in some ways, I should still be there. I should be there now, sitting high on the hog, and I would be too, if it hadn't been for Annie Bartleby. I would be.

Well. That's all under the bridge. I resigned. Far from asking me to resign, the board treated me very respectfully, gave me a small exit package that wasn't worth much, but still, it said I was valuable, and the work I had done was valuable to them. It didn't help much, but I wasn't kicked out either.

The job I have now, like Kore, is much better than what I had before at the clinic in many ways. But I didn't know that when I left. I didn't know I was going to land on my feet when it was all over, and I can tell you, if it had been up to Annie Bartleby and Harry Brice, I'd still be lying in the middle of the street, run over by the two of them. I've learned an important lesson: there are two kinds of people in the world—those who run over people and say I didn't hit them, they stepped in front of my car, and those who get run over no matter what they do.

But I know one thing—I'd rather be picking myself up over and over than being the one in the car running other people down. That's what it comes down to. What kind of person you are born to be. And I knew that, those long afternoons I talked with Barbara. I knew she was right; I had to leave. I knew it was right for the clinic. It just took a little while for me to go.

Part of the problem was that there was still so much happening with my leg and the lawsuit and all that, I couldn't concentrate on much else. But, too, I finally realized one night after Kore and I had talked and she had gone to sleep but I couldn't shut my eyes of course, was that I was waiting for something. Something, I didn't know what, when suddenly that night I realized I was waiting for Barbara to say that she'd hire an interim director and keep the job open for me until I got back on my feet. Barbara and I had already talked about how it would be good for me personally to get well and get rested before I got on with my life, and I knew she was right. I still think they could have hired an interim director, but at the time, we didn't know how long I'd be out, and Barbara seemed anxious to get someone in right away.

Well, all that's fine and good, but what I realized that night was that I didn't have any idea what *I* was going to do for a job after I got off disability and *was* able to work. Kore kept saying that it would be okay, that I could do anything, but I knew that wasn't true.

I mean, who was going to hire me? Look at me. I weighed less then than I do now. You know how it is out there. How hard do you think it was going to be to find a job for a fat, middle-aged white woman with a bad knee coming off a year's disability, with no college degree and only one real job for the last seven years? Well, would you hire her? Not likely.

Yes, I went to college, but I never finished. I went to Berkeley. Finishing just didn't seem very relevant at the time, and I always worked somewhere in the movement ever since, so it hadn't been a problem. But the years between forty and fifty are big years. I guess maybe I never thought I'd get old. There always seemed to be a job, something important to do, something I wanted to do that turned up. But you know, you get to a point where you want a few things, and you know you aren't going to be able to work forever.

Maybe that was it. I knew then that I wouldn't be able to work forever. I knew what it was like when my body gave out and wouldn't work, and I knew nothing I could ever do would bring it back. I knew I had a certain number of steps left in my body, and that after I had taken that number, my options were going to be very limited. I wanted to be very careful about where I planted my feet after that.

There is something about that, and it's not just my knee but menopause, too. It's like a big sign in the road that says, OKAY, THIS PART OF YOUR LIFE IS OVER, AND YOU CAN NEVER GO BACK. Well, I knew that a long time ago. I've had other big signs in my life that said you can never go back. Nothing like losing a parent when you are still a child to understand that. But about my own body, I guess I hadn't ever really understood that some things wouldn't be coming back.

Of course, some things I don't miss at all. I can't say I miss my period, to give you one good example. I don't miss that much at all. And I don't miss the PMS, and I don't miss the cramps, and I don't miss having to worry about the change in flow that came with menopause, and I really, really, don't miss the hot flashes and the sweating and the mood swings—or any of that.

I'll tell you what I miss. I miss believing that there is justice, that there could be justice, that lovers don't lie, and that strangers won't try to run you down. I miss that. And I miss the clinic. I miss the excitement and the feeling that we were actually doing something that mattered.

Oh, I know what I'm doing now counts. I mean, in some ways, what I'm doing now matters more than what I did at the clinic, at least in terms of how many people I'm affecting, how many people will actually benefit from the funding sources I can help allocate. It's a good job, and I'm proud to be doing it.

It's not that. It's that in the old days, when we would work together all weekend—Annie and I and some of the volunteers—we would send out for pizza after getting the billing out or after building some new piece of furniture or having a big spring cleaning, and we would be all together. I would look over at Annie, and I would raise up my beer like it was the best wine, and she would raise up her bubbly water, and the others would toast, and we would sing. And really it was the most family I'd ever had. That's what Annie Bartleby took away from me, more than the money.

I miss that feeling more than anything, more than the money, more than the clinic and the position I used to have or any of it. That's what I miss. I hate to admit that, but it's true. Of course, I have Kore now, and that's a million times better.

But even if I didn't, there is nothing now that will ever bring that feeling back. You can't go backward. I can't forget what I know about Annie. I can't get my knee back. And I can't get the clinic back, not that I want to, but I couldn't if I did, any more than I can get Duke to come back and walk through that door, though you don't know how many times I prayed for that to happen.

If praying could make things happen, that would have, because I prayed for that more than anyone who ever lived has ever prayed for anything.

There are some things that just don't come back. Some things you *can* get back. I mean, Laura Gilbert could have stopped that mediation settlement if she had wanted to, but she didn't. It's true I signed the contract, but Laura could have found a way out of it, she just chose not to. I didn't have that power. There wasn't a thing in the world I could do to defend myself then. I couldn't get my own signature back. There have been a lot of things I couldn't get back. I'll tell you one thing: I never thought I'd be fifty years old and be where I am. Never in a million years could I have dreamed this.

Laura

Well, I didn't hear from her for a week. I did hear from the mediator, who was actually a pretty nice old guy. He did, in fact, recommend about ten grand higher as a settlement. I called Margaret right away.

Took her two days to return my call, which I found less amusing than tiresome at that point. I was beginning to feel like I was in the middle of a poker match. Whether Margaret said she was a gambler or not, she was certainly acting like one. There is a time limit on these kind of things, an emotional time limit, if not one that is an actual condition of the settlement. Attorneys, better than most people, know very well that in any negotiation, the person who waits the longest often wins. In law, the way that strategy is most often countered is to withdraw the offer or make it conditional. Since this offer hadn't been made with a time condition, I was getting more worried each day about a call saying—since you're not interested in that offer, we're going to reduce it by ten grand. Obviously, that would weaken our position considerably.

That's what I was afraid of, that Margaret would wait too long, and we'd lose our advantage. So, when she finally called me back, I explained this to her in no uncertain terms. I remember she was unusually tight-lipped in her response. "Fine," was all she said. "I'll make an appointment to come down tomorrow."

I had a sinking feeling I might be in for a repeat of the previous week's exercise in off-shore dumping, but there wasn't much I could do but be prepared. After Rebecca, I generally avoid dumpers like the plague, but in my particular line of work, I didn't have much of a pool of non-dumpers to pick from. Still, Margaret was working on a top ranking.

She walked in two hours late for her appointment again, glared at me from the Queen Anne's chair we have in the reception area, and said gruffly, "Let's get this thing over with" when I came out to get her.

I didn't reply, just escorted her down the hall. She didn't speak either. I had the papers ready for her on the table in my office and gestured to them as I walked in and closed the door. She went directly over to the table, leaned over it with both hands, and said "Where's the pen?" She didn't even read the settlement contract.

"Where do I sign?" she said, as though she were signing bail to be released from an unjust imprisonment, and I were the jailer.

"Margaret," I said, having had just about enough. "Is this what you want to do or not?"

She threw the pen down on the table and turned her eyes on me.

"Is this what I want?" She gestured to her knee. "Is this what I want?" She drew her hand in an arc around the room. "What do you think I want?"

"I have no idea," I said, as calmly as I could. "But if you don't want to sign that thing, then don't. No one is putting a gun to your head."

She sucked in a long deep breath and held it, while looking up at the ceiling. God, she must have been a difficult child, I thought suddenly. What was she going to do now? Hold her breath until I change my mind? Instantly, I felt exhausted.

"I want to get this thing over with and get my life back, that's what I want," she said finally, through gritted teeth.

"Signing will get this thing over with," I said. "I don't know if it will mean you'll get your life back."

"Well, I think we already know the answer on that, don't we?" she said, hissing out the last phrase.

This time I was the one who looked out the window.

"I suggest you read it before you sign it."

"I pay *you* to read it," she answered, signed with a

flourish, threw the pen down, and walked out as regally as I'd ever seen her.

Margaret, I thought later, nursing a cold latte and watching the setting sun bathe the city in gold as opulent as the pearl gray that fills the sky in the winter. Yes, it was late. Isn't it marvelous how the sun stays so late in the sky in the summer? You just wait. It's like getting a whole other day about four in the afternoon.

Well, I had been working. Margaret wasn't my only client, and Brenna had something that night, I forget what. I try to keep up, but she's very active—square dancing, her quilting guild. I think because she works alone during the day, she likes to get out at night. It suits me fine. I don't get to see her as much as I'd like, but maybe that's not true. After all these years, maybe I do like it that way. I love for her to come home to me now, even when I'm not working late, not as often anyway.

But that night, I certainly was. It must have been about nine because I was just beginning to pack up. I didn't feel great, to tell you the truth. I would have much rather Margaret had come to terms with what had happened and the choices she was making, but some times you just can't get that from a client. You do your best, well, you've heard this all already, and I'm not sure it's not totally self-serving anyway.

I guess my point is that what had become very clear to me during the course of our work together was that Margaret wanted *someone* to pay, to pay for the great wrong that had been done her. She couldn't say this, of course, because she's not stupid and on a conscious level, she would know that it was impossible.

Don't misunderstand me. I believe a number of great wrongs *have* been done to Margaret Donovan, not the least of which was the way she lost her clinic, although I don't know that she would say that. But she was terribly wronged when

Brice hit her. We do assume that we live in a civilized country and can cross the street unharmed.

Well, I don't care. I do think he hit her, not the other way around. It's a ludicrous argument anyway. She was close enough to the crosswalk even if she wasn't, technically, in it. I hate that part of the law, missing the forest of rightness for the one little detail that might, perhaps, be wrong.

Anyway, I do believe she suffered from no fault of her own, or at least, from very little fault of her own. And for that, she deserved compensation. It's hard for me to believe that anyone who wasn't in the position of having to pay that compensation would find that not to be true.

She deserved her money. That's not the point, and it never was. I explained all this to her, sure, but it didn't matter. Because the problem did not lie there. The problem, I believe, was that Margaret wanted Brice to pay for *all* the injustice done her, and that would have been a princely sum, indeed, a sum equal to her exit. I could not get her that sum or anywhere even close to it.

And frankly, I don't know that it would have helped. Or maybe that's just self-serving, too. How many times had I had these discussions? I was exhausting even myself. God, I thought as I loaded my briefcase, and then more resolutely, but without the sense of habit I'd had loading it, I began unloading it. Why take work home? I was supposed to be winding down, wasn't I?

It was at that rather schizophrenic moment that I heard someone come in the front door. Thinking it was the cleaning man, I called out, "Hello?" I was surprised to hear Audrey call out in reply.

Soon, she came padding in, shoes held in one hand then tossed to the floor. She looked at me and smiled and said, "Boy, what a night. And I still have a brief to write!"

I put down my papers and looked at her and laughed.

"And where have you been, Missy?" I asked, coming over

to join her in the armchairs. I felt enveloped by the memory of the many nights Audrey and I had worked late or come back to the office after attending some meeting so that we could work, dishing all the way. Audrey was such a great disher that I had often thought she must have been a gay man in a previous life.

"Oh God, a meeting with Barbara Chadwick down at the Brooklyn," she said with her rogue grin. "And guess who else was there, perched on a bar stool, eating oysters and drinking champagne with her sweetie? Who was there so boisterously that the entire restaurant knew she was there and were quite happy to watch since she was so oblivious to everyone else?"

"I can't imagine," I said with a sinking feeling. "But if it's who I think it was, I hope she kept her mouth shut."

"Oh no. Oh no, no. Why would she want to do a thing like that? All I can say is, it's a good thing the Brooklyn is a straight restaurant, because girlfriend, you'll *never* get any clients from anyone who heard Margaret Donovan hold forth from the bar!"

"She should have been a lawyer," I said.

"Too easy," Audrey said, still laughing, but getting up from the chair. I could see again, like I had the million times since I had told her I was getting out of the practice of law, the shade coming down between us. We weren't to share things anymore, only memories. And I knew it wasn't her stabbing my heart, it was just that I was having that old feeling: left out, not right, not part of the crowd, never was, never would be. She certainly didn't seem to be harboring any anger, but who could tell what was under all the distance?

She got up and retrieved her shoes. "I take it you settled today," she said, looking up at me and still laughing.

"You should have seen her."

"I'm not sure I would have wanted to."

"Well, she did sign, with great unhappy flourish."

"Are they ever happy?"

"Very few. But you know as well as I."

Maybe it was something in my tone.

"God, I'm going to miss you, you insufferably correct old Yankee."

I crossed over to her. "You can't imagine how grateful I am for everything you gave me," I said, thinking that I might hug her, but pulling back, for some reason, at the last moment.

She moved away; the moment passed. "I'll have to imagine it, won't I?" She smiled, and the sting eased. She stood leaning in the doorway, her shoes held in one hand, her cheek on the molding.

"You know, there's one question I always wanted to ask you."

"Now's your chance," I said, smiling and hoping the smile masked my fear. After all the things we'd talked about, all the nights like this when we'd discussed the entire world, I had no idea what could come out of that fertile brain that she hadn't already asked me.

"What *do* you do with your feelings?"

I just stared at her. "What do I do?" I repeated stupidly. "Well, I, what do you mean?"

"Well, here we are, Barbara and I, watching Margaret having *her* feelings, at least part of some version of them, certainly in her hilarity there was fury. And I'm thinking to myself, my God, if ever there was a mismatch between attorney and client . . . And then I got to thinking, well, after all these years, that I had never seen you cry, never heard you raise your voice, and I just wondered, is this like a New England thing or what?

"Because I'm just wondering, you know? I hate to lose you. I'm just wondering if instead of walking away from all this, you might just like to get out your feelings. Most of us do, you know. You'll feel better in the morning."

I laughed weakly in relief and sat back down in my desk chair and smiled back at her.

"You've always been awfully good to me," I said, grateful once again for the way she had included me, made room for me.

"Okay," she said and sounded full of regret. I realized I was supposed to have done something other than what I did.

"Audrey," I said, trying to call her back. She poked her head around the door from the hall. "I just can't do it anymore. There really isn't more to it than that. Maybe I never should have done it."

"You're a very good lawyer."

"I may be. But I'm not happy."

"Who would know, poker-face?" I laughed in spite of the name-calling.

"I tried."

"You did better than try. You did good. Even for Margaret Donovan."

I sighed. "I'll miss you, too."

"Well, you're not leaving tomorrow are you?" She feigned distress.

"No. Tomorrow I'm going down to get this sucker recorded before anything else happens and Margaret changes her mind!"

We both laughed.

"I'm not taking any work home tonight," I said, getting up myself and retrieving my coat. "Think of that."

"Stop bragging," she called out as she went in the opposite direction down the hall.

"Good-bye," I said softly to myself. I *would* miss her, I thought as I pulled the door hard enough to latch. My hands felt empty, strange, wrong somehow. Later that night, when Brenna rubbed them for me and kissed them, she told me they would feel better later, once they knew to what use I would put them. And I thought about that—hands to lift and carry, hands to caress and love, hands to weave yarn into warmth, hands to wipe away tears, to hold a baby, a child, a partner in the night, so small our hands, so unequal to the task of providing shelter or peace for more than a moment.

And I thought about that long after Brenna was asleep that

night, how there is really so little we can do for each other to ease the pain, and I thought about it when I took Margaret's settlement agreement down to be recorded the next day.

I didn't know if I was so full of regret for Margaret or for me or for what I was losing or what I had lost or for what we all were losing every day. When I had left D.C. and Rebecca, I had left in a fog, a dense impenetrable sea of darkness. I could only see the next few steps ahead. I took them, moving against a terrible underwater current, unable to see what else might happen or how I might feel. I couldn't stop to feel. If I had stopped, I might never have gone anywhere at all. I had no idea where I was going. I was only fleeing, accepting the help of anyone who came along, and there were some whose hands I never should have taken, and there were others, like Audrey, who had held out a helping hand. Of course there were strings attached, but so what? I didn't think badly of her for that, only of myself for not being able to see more clearly ahead of myself.

This leaving felt different for me, even though I didn't know where I was going, I knew I was going *to* something, not so much away from something. I was setting out on a journey, not fleeing a war-zone. And maybe Audrey was right, maybe the war-zone was just in my heart.

But it didn't feel that way so much then. I can tell you when I took Margaret's settlement down to be recorded, I felt sad that I couldn't have done better for her. On the other hand, I did feel I had done the best I could, perhaps the best anyone could, and that I had gotten the job taken care of with a minimum amount of what my dad used to call "stuff and fuss" which, given the opportunities for drama with the situation, was somewhat of an achievement. I was not unpleased with myself.

And when it was all over, I must say, I did feel like celebrating a little myself, perhaps not down at the Brooklyn Oyster Bar, but maybe at the Sisters soup shop, maybe actually eating there instead of bringing it back to my desk. It felt like not a big achievement, but something, maybe something bittersweet. And I remember thinking over my soup that the best we could hope for from life were those bittersweet moments. I had met an artist once when I was quite young, still working corporate in D.C., who had told me that. At the time, I had looked at her beautiful, worn face and thought—not me, babe. Well, we learn, don't we?

I can tell you, that mood stayed with me for at least the next four days. I felt reflective and somewhat melancholic, but I think it was partly because the weather was changing back from gold to pearl and because all my other cases were winding down, too. The diminishing pressure gave a slightly unreal cast to the entire time, as though I were rising too quickly from the deep water and could see the light coming through the surface. It still seemed a long way away, but I could see it, and I was floating up to it, almost without will of my own anymore, as though this part of the journey were inevitable, and all I had to do was float upward.

On the fourth day, all that ended with a phone call. If I had been swimming to the surface with all my might and had gotten the bends as a result, I wouldn't have been more surprised.

It was Margaret on the other end of the line, her words slurred as they hadn't been since the previous winter. "Don't record the thing. Don't do anything. You haven't, have you?" she shouted into the phone, her voice sounding almost unfamiliar.

"Margaret?" I asked, trying to make sure, but already knowing, with a sinking heart, feeling myself being pulled back under. "What is it?"

"I fell, goddamn this knee. I fell, and it all came apart. I've just been released from that hell-hole of a hospital. Those bastards are going to have to pay for this, and you'd better make it happen for once in your life, Laura Gilbert."

"I can't," I almost whispered into the phone.

"What?" she shrieked.

"Margaret, it's over," I said, finding my voice. "It's completely out of my hands."

"You'd better get over here and explain this to me!" she shouted.

"Tomorrow is the earliest."

"Now!"

"I can't, Margaret. I'll be there tomorrow."

I hung up and sat with my head in my hands. One more time, was all I could think. One more time, and that's it. I'm done now. There was no more regret, no more bittersweet. I felt quite clear that I was done with the entire business.

After the Fall

Margaret

I wondered when this was going to come up. You must have talked with Laura recently, didn't you? Well, I'm glad to know *something* happened to her.

I never heard from the State Bar myself. I mean, I made the complaint, and I suppose I could have sued her for malpractice, but why? She didn't have any money. I just wanted to make sure she never practiced law again.

You're goddamn right I went after her. I don't suppose she told you everything that happened. Never mind. I know the answer to that. Let's try again. Would you like to hear my version again, in more detail?

I mean, I've already told you this once. In the first place, she was not good at presenting my case. Secondly, she did not care to keep at it long enough to get me adequate compensation. She didn't have the stomach for it—okay, you ask her that—you ask her if she's an attorney anymore and ask her when she made the decision to quit. I can tell you it was before me; it was long before me.

She just didn't fight for me. I'm still mad about it. Here I was, basically not able to function in my life, still on pain meds, still trying to figure out what hit me, literally. I mean, come on. I needed help. I paid for help. What I got was somebody saying to me, "Let's just get this over with."

Listen to me. She practically begged me to sign the settlement agreement. I didn't want to. I told you that. By the time I got my share, it would have been nothing. Everybody else was going to get paid first, and what was I going to get? Not enough to pay for my next knee surgery, I can tell you that.

She wanted me to sign it, and I kept thinking to myself, now what's wrong with this picture? I knew it was wrong, but she was the expert, right? And she kept telling me that it was the best we could get.

Well, maybe the best she could get. I finally got myself a real lawyer, after I got rid of her. That took a while too.

All right, that's okay. I'll start at the beginning. I've learned by now you can't follow more than one thought at a time.

It's very simple. This is what happened. We had a mediation. We got a hostile mediator, who actually asked me more questions than the opposing counsel. The opposing counsel, that was the attorney for Triple-A where cheapskate Brice had his insurance. The opposing counsel was very hostile and openly stated to the mediator that he thought my demands— my demands for compensation for my knee, remember—were excessive, although someone is going to have to explain to me what excessive might mean when you are talking about how a person moves around all day, every day.

Nonetheless, they thought my demands were excessive. Now, my attorney had already told me, in as many words, that *she* thought the amount of money we were asking for was too much, too. "I don't think this will fly," she said to me the day we were working out the dollar amounts, "but let's give it a try." That should have been my first clue, but I wasn't exactly able to judge what was going on very well at that point in my life because I had been so disabled I couldn't even work for months. I'm not an attorney anyway. That's why I hired one—because I didn't know what to do.

Are you with me so far? Am I going too fast for you? Good.

The opposing counsel said I didn't have much lost wages to worry about since I hadn't been paid that much at the clinic, completely ignoring the fact that my salary had been increasing steadily with each grant we got, and had been scheduled to increase even more if I had been able to secure the grant we were working on the day I got hit, which I wasn't. My counsel was unable to make these points for me.

There was a question of my liability. The opposing counsel said I walked into Brice's car. My counsel was unable to find a witness to say that I was in the crosswalk when I was hit nor was she able to explain to them that in Seattle, reasonable people do not walk into cars, something that seemed to have escaped all of their attention.

Then there was the issue of prior condition. Because *my* counsel had traveled to Olympia and taken a deposition from the doctor who treated me after my father's accident, we now had evidence of what the opposing counsel could call "extensive prior injury." If she hadn't been so kind, we could have just said I fell out of a tree when I was young and broke my leg, but no, I had to have Ms. Private Investigator for my attorney.

The issues of my weight and future medical care were never convincingly resolved by my counsel. There were a number of issues not convincingly resolved by my counsel. By the end of the mediation, the opposing counsel had offered me a settlement from which I would get thirty thousand dollars. That was less than Annie Bartleby took from the clinic. It was less than one total knee replacement would cost, although I didn't know that at the time. What I did know was that thirty thousand dollars wasn't enough to give me back my knee, and it was in no way what Laura kept calling "adequate compensation" for what had happened to me.

I was outraged when she told me what they had offered. Let me make something very clear to you. I remember exactly what Laura Gilbert said to me the first time she met me. She said "I'm on your side." She said, "I don't think we'll have any trouble with this." She said, "We'll get you what you deserve."

And there I was, in pain still, and my knee was aching, and I'm standing in the hall of this legal firm, and I'm listening to my own attorney present this offer to me, and I just looked at her, and I walked out. I just walked out, and I went home. I don't know what she did, and I don't really care.

She called me later and asked me what I wanted to do, and I said I wanted to think about it. She told me then that she didn't think I was going to get a better offer, and I just could not believe it. It made me crazy. I remember I talked for a long, long time with Kore about it that night, and I remember that I was afraid to go to sleep. We had had some wine to help me get to sleep, and I remember being so angry I just wanted to throw the bottle through the window; I just wanted to smash something, anything.

But I couldn't, could I? I mean, it wasn't like I could just get up and hit a golf ball again. I'll never be able to do that for the rest of my life. And I sat there, and I thought about that, and the more I thought, the angrier I got.

So, I didn't call Laura for a few days. I just didn't want to think about it, so I didn't. I tried to go about my normal day, except nothing was normal anymore. So finally, she calls me and says again that she doesn't think I'm going to get any better and that I need to make up my mind, because if I don't, the Triple-A guys are going to walk with this offer, and the next one they would make would be lower still.

So, I say okay. That's what I did. I was tired; I was so tired that I was pretty much not thinking clearly. That plus the pain meds and the pressure she was putting on me—that was one of the things I complained about to the Bar—I just caved in. I was too tired to fight anymore. That's why I'd hired her, anyway, to fight for me. And if she couldn't fight, then God knows, I couldn't either. So, I didn't. I went down to her office, and I signed.

And when Kore came home that night, I told her, and we cried. I told her how much I was hating my life, cooped up in the house all day, with no work to go to and nothing to do, and how I thought I was really going crazy. So she, she's so good to me, she suggested that we get all dressed up and go out to dinner, and I thought that was a great idea. So that's what we did, we went down to the Brooklyn Oyster Bar and ate oysters and drank champagne until I couldn't stand up. We laughed and had a good time like we hadn't in months. We took a cab home and went to bed, and I actually slept that night.

I got up in the morning, felt like hell, and wanted a shower immediately. My leg was really aching from the night before and I knew if I could just get it in the shower and let hot water beat down on it, I'd feel better.

Well, I was still not walking very well. I was still not rehabbed completely, and I slipped in the shower and blew it out. I've already told you all that. But the thing is, I absolutely would not have fallen, if my leg hadn't been so unstable from Brice hitting it. I'd never slipped in the shower before. It was completely related to the accident.

Now, as I think I've told you, I went straight to surgery, and I was in the hospital for the next three days. This was not unusual. When I got out, the first phone call I made was to Laura Gilbert to tell her not to go ahead with the settlement.

And that's when I finally woke up to the fact that I had the wrong attorney. She didn't want to stop the process, said she didn't know if she could. Well, godammit, *I* would have. I would have done anything that I could for my client.

But then, she began questioning me, like the Triple-A guys. She said to me, "Was this the morning after you had such a good time at the Brooklyn?"

Well, I was stunned. First of all, I had no idea how she knew I was there. Secondly, I certainly didn't see how it was any of her business. When I asked her that, and she said that she just wanted to know all of what was going on, I tell you then, I really didn't feel like we were on the same side. I didn't feel that way at all.

Still, she was *my* attorney. And I felt like I had spent so much time with her, and invested so much, and plus, I thought she liked me. I still had some idea in my head that she liked me, and I really believed she wanted me to get what I deserved. I couldn't believe she really wouldn't go through with refusing the offer.

"Slither out of the old agreement," is what she called it. What old agreement?—is what I wanted to know. Godammit, we didn't have an agreement. Sure, I'd signed it, but I hadn't received anything, and I didn't know squat about contracts, but I knew that from Duke—no tickee, no washee—I mean, no check, no valid contract.

But still, I couldn't quite believe what she was doing. I had been kind of uneasy with her from the start—I thought her going to Olympia was way, way out of bounds—and other attorneys told me later they thought she was too involved. I thought so, too. I felt kind of like things were never really above board with her, like she wanted something from me that I wasn't able to give. For all I know, she was attracted to me and didn't say so. I guess I should be grateful for small favors, but as I say, I couldn't really add it all up at the time.

So when she said to me that if I insisted on pursuing the matter, she thought I should have another attorney to represent me, I really couldn't believe it. I mean, who was dumping who here? It was outrageous, on top of insulting. And who was going to pay her fees, I wanted to know—who would pay? I didn't ask her that because I knew then that's why she wanted to settle. She just wanted her money and wanted to get out.

Well, fuck her, that's what I thought. I'd make her stay. She couldn't just abandon me like that in the middle of a case any more than a doctor could abandon her patients. At least, a doctor has to give a patient a thirty-day notice of intent not to render care, and if Gilbert was going to do that to me, she was going to have to pay for it, not me.

Plus, I really did not want to start over with someone new. I wanted to get it over with, too. I just wanted her to go back to Triple-A with the new information and renegotiate something. It seemed so easy to me. And if we had to go to arbitration, then we would, by God; we were more than halfway there anyway.

So then, what does she do? She takes *me* to court. I've never been so humiliated in my whole life, and I hope you write this down for your readers. Anyone who abandons a client in mid-case like she did to me deserves whatever happens to them, I mean it. It was the most cold-blooded thing I'd ever seen. She made Annie Bartleby look like a saint. She got up and said that I wouldn't take her advice, and so she couldn't provide effective counsel for me.

Well, excuse me. Who hired who to do what? I wanted to strangle her then and there on the spot, and if Kore hadn't been with me, I might have. I cursed the day I ever saw the bitch, and frankly, I was delighted by then to see her go.

I did, indeed, get other counsel, and I eventually got much closer to what I needed for my knee. I still didn't get enough, but I have an allowance for future medical care, and that's all I really wanted to begin with. I was never in it for the money, something that seemed to have escaped Laura Gilbert. I just wanted to make sure my knee was taken care of by the man who had ruined it. I don't think there's anything wrong with that and neither did the man who ended up being my attorney for the arbitration hearing.

One of the few times I have actually enjoyed working with a man. He was slimy and overreaching, and he did exactly as I wanted him to do. Get slime to hurt slime, that's what I learned from all this. After the revolution, we can talk nicey-nice about win-win situations and mediations and compromises that work out. Right now, life is not like that.

I have no regrets about any of what I did later. I am not remotely sorry about reporting Ms. Gilbert to the authorities, such as they are. There really wasn't very much I could do to her. The attorneys write the laws, and I suppose it's not surprising they had made it difficult to register complaints against their peers, but I did it, and I am not sorry.

I'm only sorry I don't know what they did to her. I hope they disbarred her, but I bet they didn't. I bet they didn't do anything, although it sounds like, at least, they notified her. And the other thing I did was, I never paid her a dime. She sent me a bill for her costs, which I found so infuriating that I just sent it back. I wrote across the top, "Go ahead, hold your breath while waiting for me to pay this."

And I never heard from her again. I hope she's doing something very, very useful with her life, like working in a relief camp in Bosnia, but I bet she's not. You know, I've thought about this a lot. I've thought about why she did what she did to me, and all I can come up with is that she must have been seriously disturbed in some way that didn't have anything to do with me. I'm not sure she had any other clients while she was working with me, and I'm not sure she had much of a law practice. I found out later that one of Barbara's good friends had been trying to keep her in practice for a long time, although why, I'm sure I don't know. She must have had personal problems.

I just wish she hadn't taken them out on me. Now. Is that what you had heard? Is that what you wanted to know? Write this down. It would take more than Laura Gilbert to stop me. I didn't get what I deserved, but I got as much as I could get, no thanks to her. People just have to stand up for themselves. It's very important. No one will just give you what you need. You have to be able to get it for yourself. And the Laura Gilberts of the world will never amount to anything more than the Annie Bartlebys because they give up too soon. They just give up, and then where are they?

Laura

I did see Margaret one more time in court, when I asked to be relieved of my duties as counsel, since I could no longer effectively advise her as my client. That whole legal maneuver is an exercise in finesse. One must speak very respectfully of one's client, while managing to give the judge the clear impression that the client is a crazy person, and you just can't help her. I had never had to do that kind of thing; neither had Audrey, but I learned, and for once, passed the information along back to her.

But that day in court, if Margaret had been anywhere near something she could have thrown herself against, she would have detonated. I knew, from our last conversation, to expect something like that, so I kept well away, as away as I could have in such a courtroom situation. And because of that, I don't count that time really as the last time I was with Margaret Donovan.

When she had called me the last time, I had promised to go over to her house, mainly to get her off the phone at the time. I needed time to think things through. It was hard to imagine something worse happening to Margaret. Well, of course there were worse things; but her timing, as usual, was awful. Did I say her timing? I don't mean that. I don't believe it was her. I mean the timing of the accident in the shower itself.

Had she been hungover from her wild night at the Brooklyn? Probably. Did it make any difference? Not one I could see. I didn't believe it was something she had done to herself deliberately, or something for which she had liability; people fall in the shower all the time. I myself have a chipped front right tooth from where I fell in the shower one night, and I was stone cold sober.

But I couldn't get the settlement changed, and I decided that night as I sat in the darkness at home watching the lights come up on Mercer Island, I decided I wouldn't try. There wasn't anything else I could do for Margaret. I had made her the best deal I could make her. That she fell later was too bad. It was a shame. But it was too late. All I had to do was explain that to her.

While I did not look forward to that, there were some places in my life where *my* word did make a difference. At least to me, it did. I couldn't knowingly lie for her. I couldn't knowingly lie for anyone anymore, not then, even if it were for all the right reasons, which it certainly would have been that time. But I couldn't do it. Margaret would have to find someone else who could. There were plenty of folks like that. God knows, the profession is full of people who knew exactly how to put just the right spin or interpretation on an event. I didn't think it would take her long to find someone else to represent her. But it would take me forever to forgive myself for doing it, and miracle of miracles, I found I still cared enough about myself not to do it. I wasn't sure how I was going to explain all that and didn't actually think I could, but I knew I was going to have to do something. On the other hand, I thought as I drove over, maybe Margaret would do something. Instead of calming me, I became more nervous thinking about just what that might be.

Kore let me in without a word. I walked to the back of the house feeling like I was headed for the Grand Inquisitor herself and getting more and more testy by the moment.

The place was worse than I had ever seen it. Strewn about were boxes with half-eaten pizzas in them and what appeared to be Chinese or Thai take-out boxes. Pizza and Asian food smells competed with one another. In addition, there was a scattering of newspapers on chairs, a footstool, the floor. A mass of tissues—used and unused, shredded and unshredded—lay on the floor next to Margaret's couch. More than the untidiness, though, and stronger than the food smells was an acrid stench of—what? Maybe medicine? The decay of a body? Or a soul? Even though I dismissed my own dramatic ponderings, the odor made my stomach clench.

And Margaret was on the couch again, the lioness pegged to a stake. Her eyes were glassy and melted down. She didn't speak as I pushed one of the cats off a chair and propped my chin in my hands.

After a long silence when she would alternately stare at me and then look out the window, I cleared my throat and said "Margaret. You asked me to come. I'm here. What is it you want?"

Suddenly, she shrieked, "I want a new settlement! That's what I want!"

The cats all jumped and stared at her. Kore poked her head in and looked at me. I couldn't tell if she was angry with me for upsetting her patient, or if she was worried about my being devoured by a wounded lion.

"Get out of here, Kore," Margaret barked at her, and I waited until the door stopped swinging before I made my reply.

"I can't do it, Margaret. The settlement has already been recorded in court."

"Well, I haven't received anything in the mail yet," she said in a very patronizing tone. "I do believe that means the deal has not yet been consummated."

"This is not a marriage bed, Margaret," I said.

"It's not a settlement either!" she roared. "Do you have any idea what's happened to me? My leg is going to be permanently crooked now, do you understand that? It's never going to be straight. I'm always going to walk with a limp. I'm never going to be able to run. And I've got seven more months of *this hell* to live in. Don't you understand anything?"

I kept my mouth shut and started counting the books in the bookshelf, but I was listening.

"Godammit, who's going to pay for all this? The clinic can't. Don't you understand? I'm going to lose the clinic."

She began to weep then, great sobbing gulps of tears. I didn't move. I waited to see if Kore would come in, but thought it understandable when she didn't.

I don't know what I expected when she was finished, but I certainly didn't expect her to turn on me again with the same ferocity.

"Can't you do something besides just sit there like a bump on a log? What do you think I pay you for, godammit? You *find* a way to get me a new settlement. You're my attorney. You have to do what I want you to do."

Margaret, Margaret, I thought to myself. You've made a fatal error here, committing your pawn to K4. I don't have to do anything you tell me to do. *You* certainly don't own me. If I wouldn't do what Rebecca wanted me to do, and I loved her, imagine what I won't do for you.

Still I didn't say a word. I couldn't translate my thoughts into speech.

"You have to do something," she said finally, her tone brisk. "I just can't tolerate this."

The words lay there between us. I believed her. And I felt badly for her.

Finally, I said, "There is one thing I can think of to do. I can resign as your attorney, and you can get someone else to represent you. Perhaps they will have better luck than I."

I stood up to leave.

"How dare you?" she hissed. "Is this what you call being on my side?"

Her face was whiter than I'd ever seen it. I began to worry about the condition of her heart, concerned if she were to stroke-out, now would be the time.

Or maybe I was just distracting myself. Her anger was so overwhelming, I hardly knew how to respond. I knew I had to be released as her counsel, but I also knew I had to get out of her house immediately.

"Margaret. I did my best as your representative. I feel it would be unethical for me to pursue your case in the manner you are suggesting."

"What exactly are you saying, counselor? That I am asking you to do something unethical? I'll tell you what's unethical. Leaving a client in the middle of a case is unethical."

She pulled herself upright, her left leg swung to the floor, and she shouted for Kore.

"And I'll tell you one other thing. I intend to take you to court for legal malpractice so fast your head will spin. You see if I don't. Kore!" she screamed again.

Kore came in, helped her up, passed her crutches to her, and together, they left the room. I had been dismissed. Fine, I thought to myself. Don't bother; I can find my way out.

I sat in the car for a few moments, shaking so hard I could hardly get my key in the ignition. As soon as I could calm myself, I drove back to the office as though it were a normal day, parked in my reserved space, went above ground to the espresso cart, got an extra tall single shot decaf, and went up to the office.

Philip handed me a very short stack of messages, which I flipped through immediately to see if either Kore or Margaret had called while I was gone. No. That meant they wouldn't. I headed back to my office. Philip called to me, "Audrey would like to see you when you get a chance."

Great, I thought. Just what I need. A little light bantering. Not now, Audrey, I thought. Not now.

I was hanging my coat up when she poked her head around the door.

"Got a minute?"

"Sure," I said. "Probably more than a minute. Sit down."

I got my latte and sat with her in the armchairs.

"Had a long morning?" she asked, looking out the windows.

"I was with a client this morning, not sleeping in, if that's what you mean. It hasn't come to that yet," I said and smiled. What was this about? Was she tracking my hours for some reason?

"I just got a call from Margaret Donovan. She wanted me to represent her in a malpractice action against you."

The room became very quiet. I could hear the phones ringing up front. Apparently, so could she.

"Tell them we're both in a meeting, Philip," she called down the hall, came back, and sat down without a word.

"Want to tell me what happened?"

"Didn't she?"

"She was somewhat vague."

"She's on a high dose of pain meds for one thing."

"She's a loose cannon on your deck, Ms. Gilbert. Better tie her down."

I got up and went to the window. Of course it wasn't going to be simple. Why was that?

"Want to tell me what happened?" she repeated.

I came back to the room, although I kept my face to the window. I couldn't quite bring myself to look at her, for some reason. "Do you remember when you saw her last week at the Brooklyn?"

"Sure I do. The sight of Margaret Donovan three sheets to the wind is not something I'll soon forget."

"Well, she went home, got up the next morning, and slipped in the shower. Landed on her knee. She just got out of the hospital yesterday. They had to totally reconstruct what they had been working on for the last eight months. She'll never be the same."

"And you've recorded the settlement."

"Correct."

"And she wants it undone."

"Correct."

"Well, legally you're covered. You don't have a problem there. But this is going to be very messy."

I turned back to look at her and pulled myself up to sit in the window well. If, in the last six years we had sat in those relative positions once, we had sat in them a thousand times. Professor and student. This time, finally, now that I was leaving, it didn't feel that way. I didn't feel anxious. I just felt sad, overwhelmingly sad.

"There isn't much I can do, except maybe step aside. Ask to be relieved of counsel. She might have a clear shot then. She could get a new attorney, denounce me to the Bar, complain about inadequate representation, she might be able to get away with it then."

"So you would fall on your sword? Why? What about your legal reputation? Are you nuts?"

"Not exactly. What's the Bar going to do anyway? Nothing. Who would take the malpractice case? Nobody but a toad, which I'm sure Margaret can find, but I'm not sure she can afford. So where are we? I'm leaving the practice of law. What would it hurt?"

She shook her head. "You are crazy. What will it help?"

"Maybe she can get more money. That's what she wants."

"And she's going to need it, too. Barbara and I were talking last week at the Broadway about how to present her situation to the board, before all this. Now, I don't think we're going to have to do much board preparation. I think if Barbara just goes to talk with her about what the clinic needs, she may be able to get her to agree to resign, but that's not going to help her with the money situation."

I turned to look out the window again, propping my head against the well wall. I suddenly felt so claustrophobic I didn't know if I could continue the conversation. I jumped off my perch and came back to the chairs.

"Audrey, don't tell me these things, okay?"

"Would you rather not know?" she asked, astonished.

"No. Now what are we going to do?" I heard the "we" in my voice and felt sickened. This didn't have anything to do with Audrey, and if I somehow made it to include her, I would have completely lost myself. "No. That's not what I mean," I interrupted her answer and continued talking until she stopped speaking and listened to me. "*We* aren't going to do anything about it," I said. "*I'm* going to do exactly what I told you. Do as you wish. Whatever you do is your own business."

She was silent and looked at me only after a long while.

"You know I will help where I can," she said finally, and got up to go. "What happened to 'we'?" she asked as she opened the door.

"I don't know," I said and heard the tears in my voice. "It's not you though; it's me." I couldn't look at her. In a moment, I heard the click of the door, and I got up, went to the window, and wept.

There was, of course, an investigation. I didn't mind that. Some guys from the Bar came over and asked me some questions, asked for supporting documents, and went on their way. I got a letter several months later clearing me of all charges, but warning me to be more careful in my dealings with my clients so as not to give even the appearance of impropriety. They assured me I was still a member in good standing.

I supposed, even at the time, that there would come a time when I would care about that, although that time has not come. At one point, Margaret accused me of losing my nerve. I thought about that a lot in the ensuing months as I looked for a job, and I suppose she may have been right.

Do you know the term? It's like when a surgeon has lost the nerve to make her first incision into someone's skin or when a gambler can't make the bluff anymore. I suppose I *had* lost my lawyer's nerve, my will to fight back, to believe I had the right to fight back in any way that it took to win. Certainly I had had that in corporate law; perhaps I even had a reputation for it. But if there had been a killer instinct in me then, it wasn't there anymore, and perhaps hadn't been since I'd lost Amanda. There were things I had done as an attorney that I could have only done from that feeling and which had relatively little to do with an actual case. They had been about me, and my feeling that I knew what was best for people, that I knew what a legal outcome should be, and by God, I could make it be that way.

If I'd felt that way before, I didn't then. And I don't know if I ever will again. Margaret was right. She did have the will to fight on. I didn't. A deal was a deal. So old-fashioned. So useless. So suddenly meaningful to me.

I retired from the practice of law in good graces with the state and, as far as I know, with my colleagues. Audrey apparently talked Margaret out of pursuing the malpractice case and helped her find someone to negotiate a new settlement. I understand she got five thousand more and her attorney got ten. Not bad, I suppose, if you're counting those things.

But I wasn't anymore. I was done.

As We Are Now

Margaret

Okay, here's the thing I want you to understand. This is our last meeting, right? And you think you understand the real Margaret Donovan, and you have enough material for your story, whatever that is by now. And you think you have the complete picture. Okay, fine.

But I don't. I don't think you have the whole picture. You are making it out to sound like I'm this sad loser, this victim. I just want your readers to know one thing. I don't want anyone's sympathy. I never did want anyone's sympathy. I didn't need that then, and I don't need it now.

I've done just fine, thank you. I absolutely landed on my feet. What can you say? That I had a hard time? True. So do most people. Mine was a little tougher than most, but so? I built a great health clinic for women that is thriving today. I built it, and when it was time for me to go, I left. I got on with my life, which is more than I can say for whoever started you on this story.

I got on with my life. Do you understand what that means? The past is past. I have a responsible job in city government, a job in which I am responsive and can make the city responsive to the needs of women. I live my life in a quiet, orderly way. I participate in my community, where I both contribute and receive from that community. I have friends, good friends, friends of twenty years or more. I am a homeowner. I vote and I keep up with the issues of the day which affect all of us. I have a happy and complete relationship in which I do not feel humiliated.

Does that sound like a loser to you? I'll tell you what a loser looks like. She looks like Annie Bartleby. I saw her last week. Did she tell you? Do you think I don't know you are interviewing her, too, as well as Laura? You surprised me last week about Laura. I mean, I know I had given you her name and a release, but since you didn't tell me anything about it, I just assumed you hadn't. But that's okay. It's just your job, right? Well, I don't know what happened to Laura Gilbert, but I'll tell you one thing about Annie Bartleby. The years have not treated her well. Talk about a victim.

I didn't recognize her. And it has only been four years since I last saw her. I haven't gone out of my way, believe me. It's a big city, but I know she's stayed out of my way, because I never see her in the places we used to go together. That's why I was so surprised to see her last week. She was in my neighborhood.

I was walking down the street, such as I walk now, going slowly with my cane, and I was talking to Kore. We had just been out for some supper and were going home to watch the game. Have you caught any of the season so far? I'm telling you, we're going for the pennant this year. The way they've restructured the league, we really have a chance now. No two-bit team is going to take it away from us this year. You really should watch some time; it's so much fun. Oh God, you can hoot and holler and scream during the exciting times and relax as the grass grows during the shut-outs.

Hoot and holler. An Annie phrase if I ever heard one. Yes, she still stumbles around in my brain a bit, the way she did when she drank. Sure, I remember all that. I was with her the first year she got sober. It wasn't very pleasant, and I can tell you being away from me hasn't done her any favors either.

She looked terrible the day I saw her, all thin and dirty. She actually looked dirty, like she'd been playing in the dirt or something. Gray hair hiding under some kind of baseball hat, her face all pinched, wasn't much to look at, I'm telling you.

Well, I saw her, and I almost walked right by her. I saw her and she registered as someone I knew, but I didn't know who exactly she was. I couldn't place her; she looked so different. And so I smiled, thinking she was someone from the clinic, and then, just as I was about to walk past her, I realized who she was. And then I did just walk right past her.

I didn't say a word. I didn't stop. I didn't look at her. I just walked right by, turned to Kore, and started talking about the game. And you know what? I was fine. I was glad I did it. I have nothing to say to that woman. Nothing.

I have nothing more to say to her than I have to Laura Gilbert, for that matter. Did you find out what the State Bar did after my complaint? I hope they showed her professional peers exactly what she was like to her clients, and that some of them, if there are any good ones, which I haven't found, shunned her. I've heard she doesn't practice anymore. Well, that's one good thing to come out of all this.

Okay, here's my latest lawyer joke. What's the difference between a dead lawyer in the middle of the road and a dead snake in the middle of the road? The snake has brake skid marks in front of it.

I can tell you one thing. I doubt that for all her high-minded talk about justice, no one gave Laura Gilbert a going-away party when she left her job.

Me? I got a big party, testimonials, catered food, the whole nine yards when I left the clinic. Actually, they waited until I was well enough to come. I guess it was about six months later that it happened.

The new director hosted it as a way, probably, of introducing herself to the community. She was from New York, didn't know anyone here, and was probably sick to death of people asking about me and where I had gone and all that sort of thing. I hadn't been back to the clinic since she'd gotten there. She was probably hoping for introductions to people, which I did provide.

Oh, I didn't care. She needed the introductions, and believe me, I didn't suffer by comparison. One of these reed-thin women, tight as a drum, downtown-looking corporate types. If I hadn't known better, I would have said she was one of the doctors.

Well, you saw her. She was at that "Honoring Our Mothers" fundraiser where you first met me. That was the only other time I've been to the clinic since I left, and I'm sure they're doing fine now with her. And, I must say, she knows how to throw a good party, although I wondered who was paying for everything. Part of me felt like that money should have been used for the clinic. We never did things like that in the early years; we couldn't afford to. But things are easier now, I guess. Takes money to make money; that's what Duke always said. And it's always harder in the beginning when you have none.

But my party, the party for me when I left, was nice. Not too big, not too gaudy like this other one. People just came by and said wonderful things about me and how much the clinic owed me and all that sort of thing. I'll tell you, it was the only time in all my years there I ever heard any of the docs say anything nice about me, and even then it was backhanded. "Couldn't have done it without me," that sort of thing. Just makes me wild whenever they say something like that. They just can't do it, can't be out of the limelight for a second, can't give anyone else credit for anything. But that's okay. Everyone else knew.

So, it was nice. Barbara Chadwick had orchestrated the whole thing, I'm sure. She always takes care of things so nicely, always makes sure people get the recognition they deserve. We had champagne and white wine and some non-alcoholic stuff, God knows we couldn't be politically incorrect. I had a good time. Kore helped me find a really nice black rayon outfit, which I wore with a bright red blouse and my red earrings, and I felt like a million bucks, except by the end of the evening when I had to sit down, but even then, people came up to me and spoke with me, actually sought me out to tell me how important the clinic was, and it helped.

It helped a lot. It wasn't enough for all the years of work and all the pain and suffering, but it helped, and I felt better about leaving. I'll tell you what, I wouldn't have been able to go to the "Honoring Our Mothers" thing without the good feelings from that going-away party. I had been thinking about not going to the fundraiser. I knew it would raise a lot of money for them, but it seemed like such a different time in my life, and I wasn't sure I wanted to visit again. Still, after I was there, I was glad I went. I was sorry the next day, both my knee and an upset stomach, but Kore and I just lounged around and read the paper and went back to bed in the middle of the afternoon. And I thought about how I was able to do that now, when I never could have done it if I had still been at the clinic.

You remember that song from *The Wizard of Oz*, where they get up late and go home early and take a long lunch and you realize by the end of the song they haven't been at work at all? That's what my Sundays are like now. I actually get to rest. I have my little golf computer game that I like to play, a little hand-held thing, and Kore cooks up a big meal, and we usually have a nice bottle of wine, and sometimes we'll watch a ball game we video-taped from earlier in the week, or sometimes we just sit and read our murder mysteries. Occasionally, we'll junk out on TV trash but not too often. Mostly, we're just an old married couple, enjoying ourselves and our lives.

Sound like a loser to you? Sound like a victim? I think not.

You should have been here last Sunday. Kore cooked pot roast and made some mashed potatoes, and God, it was good. We ate in the middle of the afternoon, just when I like to, and then we were watching a game and Kore had gotten me one of those dark chocolate bars—you know the kind, big, thick slab of chocolate—and I was eating it slowly, savoring it, and it was almost gone, and she took the wrapper, which had some flakes of chocolate in it, and she raised it up to her mouth and licked it slowly, like a cat, watching me the whole time, and I'm telling you, it was the sexiest thing I'd ever seen her do.

It was like the old days when she would do the most outrageously seductive things and then watch me while she did it, and I wouldn't be able to move because of my damn knee, and I would just watch her and just about die wanting her. And just like always, she eventually came close enough for me to grab her and pull her on top of me and then, well, it was like the old days. Not bad for old married folks.

Yeah, sure sounds like I can't have a good relationship, doesn't it? Poor old Margaret.

And you've seen my house, haven't you? Of course you have, when you first interviewed me. Now that's a real tragedy. I live in a really nice, small but really nice, house which I own. I live in a nice community where other lesbians live. My partner likes to work in the yard, and I am able to cultivate my roses without having too much strain on my knee.

I was lucky to have been able to find a nice home in a nice part of Fremont, a home with the main bedroom on the first floor, with a full bath on the first floor, so I don't have to walk up any stairs. I have three cats, and they have a yard to play in. I have a flowering apple tree in my backyard, and my neighbors aren't too loud, and I don't have to fight for a parking place, ever. I make enough money that we can afford to have a very anal-retentive faggot come in and clean once a week.

Yes, I would definitely say that this is a terrible life, and I have been a failure, wouldn't you? Sure looks like it to me.

Look, I don't want anyone to feel sorry for me, that's the main thing. And I really want people to know that I did nothing wrong, honestly. I was gullible; I trusted the wrong people, and I had some bad luck. But I've had some kind of bad luck most of my life and so have most people. It's not the cards you get dealt that are the issue; it's what you do with them that counts. That's what Duke always said, and it's what I believe to this day.

The day she left me, Annie Bartleby said she was sorry and that she knew I was going to have a tough time without her and that she had stayed as long as she could, but that she had to leave and live her own life.

God, it makes me mad even to repeat it to you now. The arrogance! I can't tell you how many times I've thought about that level of arrogance in the past four years. Somebody needs to tell that woman to get a real life.

I needed her? I don't think so. Let's look at that again. Where is she now? Look at where I am. You think I'm happy? You bet I am. Sure, I have some problems, but so does everybody. My knee is a problem and is going to continue to be. But that's not my heart. My heart is fine. And I finally got enough money to at least take care of the knee somewhat. I have a few more years. And I'm planning. I'm doing the planning I need to do to take care of myself, which is what I've always done. I've taken care of myself, and if Annie Bartleby told you any different, she has a very limited grip on reality. Maybe she's the one who's been spreading all that gossip about the settlement money.

People want to know about the money, that's fine. Tell them they can have all the money I got off the settlement if I can have their good knees. Seriously. I'd trade in a New York minute. I'd trade faster than George Steinbrenner. Oh, never mind.

Look. You go find out if Annie Bartleby or Laura Gilbert is happy. And then you come back to me and tell me. Or don't. Just tell your readers. I don't care, myself, what happens to them, I really don't. But if Annie Bartleby is in a good relationship where she is happy and settled, I'll eat my cane. I know that woman. She's never going to be happy. And Laura Gilbert? Who cares what happens to her?

The past is past. People—no, I should say lesbians—lesbians should be aware that lesbians steal from one another, that they don't tell the truth, that the community is not all it's cracked up to be, and that you have to watch who you hire and who handles the money at community institutions. That's the lesson from all this.

The other lessons are just life lessons, you know? Interview more than one attorney before you hire her. Get more than one reference. Pay attention when your lover starts saying she's bored with her life. She may be saying she's bored with you. If you are the marrying kind, find someone else who is, too. Don't stay with someone who can't make a commitment to you.

These are simple things, probably too simple for a reporter. No, you like the big, juicy stories, the big drama. But there's no drama here. Nothing terribly different or too exciting. Mostly things have just stayed the same in my life, and that's how I like it. I like peace and simplicity, and I don't like drama. I'll leave the drama to you and your readers. I don't need it. I need a quiet life with a loving woman, which is what I have now.

Terrible thing, isn't it? Don't you just feel sorry for someone like me? Well, you just make sure you tell them all of this story. Make sure you tell them where I ended up, because if you just show them the bad times, they're never really going to understand Margaret Donovan. I've survived worse than this.

I'm fine now. The past is past. I've gone on. Save your sympathy for someone who really needs it, a Bartleby or a Gilbert, don't waste it on me. I don't need it, thanks. Honestly, I don't know why I talked with you in the first place.

Laura

Well, you came to talk with me about Margaret Donovan, and I'm afraid I've told you more about my life than hers. I hope I've been helpful. I had no idea I had so much to say about any of this, and I certainly hope I didn't bore you with all the extraneous details about my own life. Mostly, I'm sure you gathered, I don't often talk much about myself. I don't know what happened this time. Maybe because the story wasn't about me, it gave me some kind of freedom. I hope you don't print it all! Well, no, I don't mind. I didn't say anything I regret, and it's all true. Sad, but true.

Yes, I still think of Margaret from time to time. All of this, obviously, still has great electricity for me. Of course, I think of her. I hope she's happy. I would like for her to be; I always wanted that. I hear about her from time to time. Sometimes I make it up to Seattle and have lunch with Audrey; we gossip mostly, like people everywhere, except now they call it networking. But I don't hear much. Audrey either doesn't hear much about her or she doesn't pass the news along. Maybe she's afraid it will hurt me.

But it won't. I don't mind. I didn't even mind the Bar investigation. I'm sure from Margaret's perspective, it was all justified. I could sit here and say her perspective was—maybe still is—distorted, but what will that really tell you? That she and I don't agree? You already know that. Is that so bad? We can disagree. There doesn't have to be a war over it.

And I don't think Margaret wants war anyway. She just wants what she wants, like the rest of us. Margaret is a little more tenacious than most, but maybe she balances out someone like me. Maybe that's not fair to me; I don't know.

My overwhelming feeling for Margaret was that she got screwed, and what I did for her only made things worse. I have many feelings of regret—not for what I did or didn't do—but for what happened and how she couldn't resolve it to her satisfaction. On the other hand, I suppose I'm holding her to a higher standard than most people ever reach. I know, myself, how difficult it is to resolve even little heartaches, never mind the big ones.

You know what I think now, really? I think this is how life is. We want our lives to be neat and tidy like a movie. In a movie, all the dead bodies get dragged away. And maybe because we see it that way so often in movies, we think life should be that way for us and think there's something wrong with us, something to be ashamed about if our lives aren't all wrapped up with a bow.

But tidy is not how life is for most of us. For most of us, the dead bodies of our lives live with us, within us, around us, in our closets, waiting to fall out, heavy as caskets, when we least expect it. And those bodies aren't all from childhood; there are some fresh corpses in there. You can't just tie your life up with a bow. If we could do that, we could learn how to tie our hearts up so they wouldn't break anymore.

Most of us, I think, if we consider these things at all, think about dead bodies in terms of our childhoods; certainly that's what the media and the self-help folks talk about. But the idea that life as an adult may be sometimes out of our control, now that's a different story. Talk about frightening! It's much too frightening to think there might be things that happen to us as adults that we might not be able to control or absorb and come to terms with. When we're children, things are done to us, and we are victims because we are little and powerless. We like to think that's not true of us as adults.

Maybe we have to believe that to go on. But it hasn't been true for me. It wasn't true for Margaret. And there aren't too many places to put such frightening feelings. Is it an accident that the movie where the dinosaurs come back uncontrolled is the highest grossing movie ever? Well, and what did Margaret read? Murder mysteries. By definition, books in which the murderer is caught and life gets back under control. We like those books; they reassure us about that big thing behind us casting such a large shadow over our lives. Maybe if we don't look at it, it will go away. Maybe someone else will catch the murderer. If not the police, then some nice lesbian detective who's funny and sexy and smart. Very smart. And in control. Our lives as virtual reality.

So, we load up our senses and our minds and our schedules, and we do something else while we're waiting for life to go away or go do whatever it's going to do to someone else. And we get to the end of our lives, and we wonder what happened, where it all went. If life does intrude on our lives, if for some reason our protections as Americans, as people for whom antibiotics still work, if for some reason, our bodies are invaded by a virus no one can cure or a cancer that no one can stop or a child or loved one is taken from us before we are ready to say good-bye or a car comes out of nowhere and hits us, well then, what do we do? We haven't much practice dealing with it, have we?

That's all I'm trying to say. I liked Margaret Donovan. Sure, she made me mad plenty of times, but that's okay. I'm still sorry for what happened to her. And not just her knee. I heard from Audrey, after I had petitioned the court to be relieved of my duties as counsel, that Margaret had been eased out of the clinic, and that seemed to me to be the final blow but maybe not. A few months ago, I saw from a fundraising letter that she was being honored at a benefit dinner as one of the clinic's founding mothers. I assume that meant she agreed to participate, so maybe there, too, she never knew what hit her. I don't know.

Maybe she still doesn't know that the day she let Barbara Chadwick control her board was the day she lost her clinic. Maybe she knows and doesn't care. I would like to know she's happy, though.

Say, you know who I play chess with on a regular basis

now? Dr. Lennox. Remember him? Margaret's old doctor? Well, when I moved down here to take the arts administrator job, I looked him up. He was delighted to hear from me. We have a wonderful time once a week. Brenna formed a new quilting group here (Olympia is just full of artists; it's amazing), and his wife has a Ladies of the Church meeting every Wednesday night, so I drive up to Shelton, and we play. Oh, I have a great time. And he's really taught me a lot. Now, when Nettie comes down for the weekend, she brings the boys who are old enough to keep themselves occupied for a couple of hours, at least long enough for us to have a game, and I've actually beat her a couple of times. A very heady experience after all this time, let me tell you!

I like my job very much. Well, for one thing, I'm working mainstream now. If people hate lawyers, they mostly keep it to themselves. They don't see me as a lawyer; they see me as an administrator, and that helps. I can just say I have my J.D. if it seems like it will be useful, and mostly people are very nice about it. Quite a switch for me.

Well, I don't know how much of it is working mainstream again or working in government or working in a transient kind of town or what. I don't know. I like it that not everybody knows my business, and it's nice to be able to meet a new group of people and not be worried about a lawyer joke someone will inevitably make.

Why is it in the lesbian community, we treat our professional women so badly? If they aren't perfect—and who is?—why, we just crucify them. I'm not talking about myself now, I mean all the doctors, the lawyers. Is this how it is in mainstream culture? I don't think so. We go after them, and I've done it, too. Is it because we don't have enough of them, that there isn't enough of a selection to be forgiving? Is it that we want so much from each other, a sanctuary, that we can't bear the slightest disappointment? We just cut each other no slack. Is it just the anxiety and brutality we develop from our constant experience of oppression? Or is it that we're all women, and women are so damaged in our society? I just don't know, but it's not very commendable for us, as a community. I don't see straight people doing this to each other. And when I was in law school, I never thought I was going to be hated in my own community or ridiculed for what I did—the sidelong glances, the interrupted conversations, the overheard jibes—"Oh, you know, she's an attorney; that's how they are."

Well? How are we? What is it about the least little bit of perceived power that makes us so want to tear each other down? I do think most people hate lawyers, and I think it's because we usually come into their lives when something very private, some very small, scared part of us has been hurt, and if our attorney doesn't fix it, we hold her responsible for the entire pain. Why is that?

Plus, there is the perception that attorneys make a lot of money, and for what? It's not like I put a cast on someone's leg that you can see and touch and hear come stumping down the hall. We don't cure anyone, so our billable hours look very different. What product do we have to offer? The whole idea is confusing to me, when approached from that angle, and I can only assume it's confusing and angering to others. I can tell you, it's a relief to introduce myself as an arts administrator.

The conversations after that are fairly predictable, depending on the political orientation of the person I've been introduced to. But every now and then, I get introduced to a real person (usually an artist) who actually asks interesting questions, like "how can I apply for a grant?" I really like helping people get money. Oh, there are the tedious parts, certainly, and the sniffy dowagers and the drooling Radical Right around my neck. I get away with surprising amounts of fun here. I love working with the artists; I get home at a reasonable hour, and some people actually think I'm doing a good job. I can still hardly believe this is my life, even after three years of doing it.

What I love most about it is the art. I'm such a fan. You know, some people think we should all be artists, but not me. What would they do without someone to admire their work? And I do. We can't all sing in the choir. Actually, I can't sing at all. Same problem. Just not a creative bone in my body. But I love to go listen. I finally found a church here; it's a little Christ-centered, but I can live with it, and they seem to be able to live with my lesbianism, so I think we're all right with each other. And the singing, oh! They sing right over my tears into my heart. Oh, I still cry; I'll never stop missing Amanda. I still miss lots of things. But that's okay. I go every Sunday, have my little cry, and come home feeling refreshed.

If Brenna's not working, we might take the kayak out and paddle around in the rain. Well, it's certainly not where I expected to be, but it's a life. And it's mine. And I can't say I'm unhappy. I don't know that I'll be here forever—certainly not if another Republican is voted into office—but for now, well, we'll just see what comes around the bend.

So, there I go again. You know, I've been mixing up Reagan and Nixon in my mind. It's funny isn't it? When Nixon died, there was an article on the front page of the paper that started out, "Only the old and the middle-aged remember hating Richard Nixon." I had to laugh. At last, I had gotten confirmation of my place in life. Well, that's where I am: middle-aged, a little thickening around the middle, and in the middle of a new career. I don't mind it much. I have a lot of regrets, but none I can't live with anymore.

I do think about Margaret. I wish things could have been different. Oh, that she would have fallen earlier or called me earlier or something. Or maybe that the crosswalk question hadn't been there. Or even that I hadn't ever drifted into personal injury work to begin with. I don't know.

In the end, it's what happened. And I can live with it. Margaret screamed at me once, "You don't know what it's like to live with this leg!" And of course, she's right. I don't have any physical problems, other than the occasional hot flash, but I don't mind that much. I don't know what it's like not to have my body work, and I can tell you, I would hate it. Brenna and I have been playing some tennis these days, and I've been practicing by myself. Those mornings alone would be difficult to give up, especially since having found it again after such a long time of ignoring my physical self. And maybe I only did that when I realized I had something not everyone had, a body that worked. I still understand I have no idea what it's like to live with daily pain and disability. So, maybe it's easy for me to say that I can live with my life.

When Margaret's doctor told me during her deposition that Margaret would almost certainly have at least intermittent pain laterally, I asked her what it would be like to live with that, and she replied "Not pleasant." Of course, opposing counsel countered later, asking if it wasn't like the occasional headache, and the doctor said "No, because some part of you always knew it was coming."

I thought about that for a long time afterward. I imagine that Margaret's pain is probably not intermittent now, but rather more regular since her last reconstruction. I try to imagine it, and I ask myself if I did the best I could, and I have to say "yes."

But of course, that's not really enough, is it? Margaret's greatest strength in building that clinic was her tenacity. She never let go. Maybe she can overcome this, too. I didn't see much of that toward the end, but people can change direction, can't they? Well, it does happen. Look at me.

But you didn't come here for that. Let me let you go. Come down and do a story on some of my artists here. Now *there* are some women who have done interesting things with their lives. You know, I just realized. You've never been down here during the summer, have you? You should see the sky when the sun's out in the summer. You've heard that expression "the sky's the limit?" On a clear day here, Mount Rainier looks like it's in your backyard, and the sky surrounding it is so blue and so endless, you might think it wouldn't take much to rise up in it and fly away into some limitless cobalt future. The mountain is huge, just rising up out of nowhere, and it doesn't show itself except on clear days. It's as though it hadn't been there at all before, but now it is, and anything seems possible.

Of course, life's not like that, but Olympia on a summer day sure makes you feel like it could be. And I think that's worth having in my life, at least with everything else. Maybe I have developed some kind of capacity for hope. You see? You never know. Thanks for coming by.

More Spinsters Ink Titles

Spinsters titles are available at your local booksellers or by mail order through Spinsters Ink. A free catalog is available upon request. Please include $2.00 for the first title ordered and 50¢ for every title thereafter. Visa and Mastercard accepted.

Spinsters Ink
32 E. First St., #330
Duluth, MN 55802-2002
USA

218-727-3222 (phone)   (fax) 218-727-3119
(e-mail) spinster@spinsters-ink.com
(website) http://www.spinsters-ink.com

Spinsters Ink was founded in 1978 to produce vital books for diverse women's communities. In 1986 we merged with Aunt Lute Books to become Spinsters/Aunt Lute. In 1990, the Aunt Lute Foundation became an independent nonprofit publishing program. In 1992, Spinsters moved to Minnesota. Spinsters Ink publishes novels and nonfiction works that deal with significant issues in women's lives from a feminist perspective: books that not only name these crucial issues, but—more important—encourage change and growth. We are committed to publishing works by women writing from the periphery: fat women, Jewish women, lesbians, old women, poor women, rural women, women examining classism, women of color, women with disabilities, women who are writing books that help make the best in our lives more possible.

Photo by Geoff Manasse

Jean Swallow was a lesbian-feminist writer, editor, and journalist whose writings were widely published in gay, lesbian, and feminist periodicals. She was the author of *Leave A Light On For Me*, editor of two anthologies: *Out From Under: Sober Dykes and Our Friends* and *The Next Step*. She collaborated with Geoff Manasse on a book of photos and interviews, *Making Love Visible: In Celebration of Gay and Lesbian Families*. In 1986, Swallow received an Outstanding Achievement Award from the National Gay & Lesbian Press Association. Jean Swallow committed suicide in 1995. She was 42 years old.